machine embroidery
for babies & tots

marie zinno

©2007 by Marie Zinno

Published by

kp krause publications

An Imprint of F+W Publications

700 East State Street • Iola, WI 54990-0001
715-445-2214 • 888-457-2873
www.krausebooks.com

Our toll-free number to place an order or obtain a free catalog is (800) 258-0929.

The following trademarked terms and companies appear in this publication:

Floriani Fusible Interfacing, KK 2000®, Pellon®, Perfect Placement Kit, Target Stickers, Therm O Web Heat'nBond®, Velcro®

Library of Congress Control Number: 2007923002

ISBN-13: 978-0-89689-558-4

ISBN-10: 0-89689-558-0

Designed by Katrina Newby

Edited by Erica Swanson

Printed in China

Acknowledgments

When I was first asked to write this book, I was shocked and flattered. I knew I had many creative and unique embroidery projects in my head, but making and writing about each one was a different story. My husband Doug is always so supportive of my craft and growing business. He knew I could run my business, design the embroidery designs, sew and embroider all the projects as well as write my Designs articles and weekly Ann the Gran projects. I can't leave out my Design-a-Purse parties and all the orders. We are talking multi-tasking to the max! Our two children, John age 12 and Lindsey age 9, are very proud of my accomplishments. Without all of their help, this book would still be a dream. Thank you so much.

I also want to thank my sister Eileen for always pushing me to think big. She has always had big plans, and it has worked for her. We love working together, mostly by cell phone. I actually commute with her each morning, even though I live in Ohio and she lives in Dallas! Technology is wonderful; it allows us to constantly bounce embroidery ideas back and forth.

My entire family has been an inspiration for this book. My parents, Pat and Betty Ward, have always supported our decisions in life and gave us an exciting and beautiful childhood at the New Jersey shore. The beach is a part of me that will never go away, even though I live in Ohio. The nautical designs in this book were inspired by the time spent there. While I was growing up, my father piloted an antique Stearman bi-plane, another source of design inspiration. Growing up in a large family with my five sisters — Mary Pat, Liz, Eileen, Kathleen and Theresa — we all managed to find a creative outlet in some way. I think we inspire each other. I love you all.

32   54   36

Table of Contents

Introduction

Machine embroidery has turned a hobby into an addiction with me. I love creating and designing projects for other embroiderers who feel like I do. When you are excited about a particular interest, it is easy to share with others, so I am so glad this book opportunity arose. I hope you enjoy making these projects for a special baby or toddler's room. The embroidery designs are very versatile. Different color combinations can alter the entire look of the room. Experiment and have fun creating! There are no wrong answers with your personal style.

While writing for Designs in Machine Embroidery Magazine, I have learned so much about embroidery. I am lucky to have access to many designs and software at my fingertips. Beautiful designs are everywhere; all you need is the inspiration to get started!

Embroidering for babies and children is inspiring in itself. Every time I embroider for a new baby, I hope that the blanket or teddy bear will be their favorite. I love to hear from people how much their baby loves that particular gift.

I know you will constantly look for store-bought blanks to use for embroidery. You can find excellent blanks in most large retailers or online. Specialty linen stores are also a good resource. I generally look in the home accessories and laundry/storage aisle. Ready-made products save time and leg work. Add a monogram or theme design from my collection, and turn a blank into a beautifully embroidered accessory. Look for blanks that will be easy to hoop and do not have too many seams, buckles or zippers. Some blanks can be taken apart to hoop and quickly re-sewn.

Shop for blanks at resale shops; you can save a lot of money and find all sorts of different blanks. This can be a good start to practice on ready-made clothing, because if mistakes do happen, it is nice to know that you did not pay full price for the garment.

The twenty embroidery designs I created are simple, but very versatile. It was exciting to stitch out the designs for the first time; it was like the designs came to life. The four themed designs contain two embroidery groupings for girls and two for boys, with an appliqué design in each category. The embroidery designs are on the CD included with the book.

getting started

Chapter 1

Working with Stabilizers

There four main types of stabilizers used for embroidery: cut away, tear away, wash away and heat away. There are many different weights and properties within these four groups.

Cut Away

This stabilizer is perfect for any fabric that has stretch. It is an easy rule to remember — if it stretches, cut it away. There are many textures and a variety of weights of cut-away stabilizer.

Match the stabilizer to the fabric weight. If you have a lightweight pique golf shirt, for example, use a poly-mesh cut-away stabilizer. The design might be a bit dense for one piece of poly mesh, so use two layers together. Poly-mesh cut-away stabilizer is available in three colors to match the shirt fabric: white, natural (beige) and black.

Comfort is important to the wearer, so think about the wearer when embroidering. Think of how the garment will be worn. If it will be worn without a shirt underneath (for baby onesies, sweatshirts, golf shirts, etc.), use a stabilizer that will not irritate the skin. Iron on a soft, fusible interfacing to the back of embroidery stitches, if needed.

Cut-away stabilizer also comes in a fusible. Follow instructions for all stabilizers as directed by the manufacturer. Keep all information taped to the inside roll of the stabilizer when the package is opened.

Tear Away

The most common and least expensive type of stabilizer is tear away. Be frugal with your stabilizers. Reuse excess pieces, and keep a container or box near your embroidery machine for scraps. Recycle when you can — it is clean paper, and you can shred it or put with office junk mail. I hate to throw clean stabilizer in the trash!

There are many tear away stabilizers as well: light weight (used for linens and light weight fabrics), medium weight (home decorating projects and bags or purses), and heavy weight (towels, thick fabrics or a very dense design).

If in doubt, do not tear away. Use a cut-away stabilizer if you are not sure of the fabric's content, or if the tear away does not cleanly pull away.

Wash Away

Wash-away stabilizer is a wonderful invention. Have you ever talked about embroidery with someone who is not an embroiderer? If you mention "wash-away" products, they suddenly become very interested. We really do use some high-tech products (not just the machines). My daughter likes to make my water-soluble stabilizer disappear for her friends by squirting a scrap pile. Nine-year-olds are very impressed with that trick!

Use wash-away stabilizers for a topping (to keep the pile from poking through the stitches) and as a backing (such as free-standing lace).

Wash-away stabilizer comes in many types, including sticky-back film, paper, woven and plastic film. It can be stuck on, ironed on and placed directly under the garment. Test the stabilizers and follow manufacturer's directions. You will find your own favorite and master the technique. I generally use wash-away stabilizer as a topping for fleece blankets, terry cloth, sweatshirt material and any thick fabric that will look better if a topping is used.

Heat Away

This type of stabilizer is used for materials that should not or can not get wet, or for especially delicate fabrics. The stabilizer is heated with a dry iron and actually crumbles away.

Keep a diverse selection of stabilizers on hand. You never know when an interesting project will pop up and you will need of a specific stabilizer. I like to store my rolled stabilizers in a wine rack — it keeps the stabilizer organized and prevents it from rolling off the counter.

Tape the packaging label to the inside of the roll for future reference.

Templates

You will see reference to templates throughout this book. I constantly use templates for laying out my designs. Templates are your actual embroidery design printed on tracing paper or transparency paper. The transparencies can be very expensive, and it takes awhile for the ink to dry. When printing on the tracing paper, it must be trimmed to fit in most printers. Tracing paper is 9" x 12" so it is one more step to trim the paper. I use a small scrapbooking tool that trims the paper quickly and easily.

Printing the template can be accomplished with your embroidery editing software, all brands should be capable of doing this. The printed version usually contains the following information: stitch count, color chart or sequence, exact measurements and file name. The grid has vertical and horizontal dotted lines. The intersection of the lines is the center of your design. Templates provide perfect placement of an embroidery design. The design will stitch exactly where you want it to when using a template.

Many embroiderers do not print templates for their projects; they just "know" where their embroidery design is going to stitch. However, guessing is not an accurate way to embroider. Plan your project and print out a few templates, and your designs will be exactly where you want them to be. You can even save the templates for the next time you use the design. Keep templates in a clear folder for future use.

Target Stickers

One of the most helpful tools for embroidery is the target sticker. Templates are a good start, but you have to be able to mark the center of the design accurately; Target Stickers do just that. They are small, white pressure-sensitive dots with crosshairs printed on them. An arrow is used to determine the top of the design. The Target Stickers are placed in the center crosshairs of the design under your template. By using the transparent tracing paper, you can see underneath the paper to the fabric. The Target Stickers work with your templates. Place the target sticker under the template. Place the sticker in the exact center, and remove the template. The needle should hit the exact center of the crosshair; remove the sticker before you hit start. You can use multiple Target Stickers on a project.

Target Stickers were created by Designs in Machine Embroidery Magazine and can be purchased directly from them (see resources).

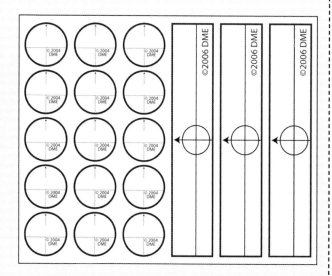

Perfect Placement Kit

This tool is another invention from Designs in Machine Embroidery Magazine. It is a combination of 15 different clear, heavyweight plastic templates, along with Target Stickers and a reference booklet of stabilizer recommendations to help embroiderers with design placement. A large envelope-style folder holds the booklet, stickers and all of the templates. For this book, I used a number of the templates and many, many Target Stickers.

The Perfect Placement Kit is available from Designs in Machine Embroidery Magazine as well.

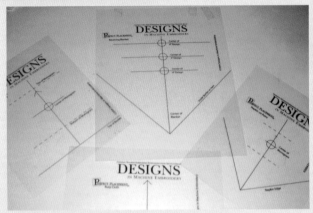

Organizing Designs

There are so many beautiful and cheap designs to collect that you will probably need an organization system to keep track of them. Having a large collection of thousands of designs is not helpful if you can't find the designs on your computer.

I like to keep all of my CDs and floppies (these will be extinct shortly) in a three-ring binder. I purchase transparent pages to hold CDs and floppy disks from an office supply store. I also keep templates of the designs I will be using in a clear folder along with the package envelope to view the actual design.

Today most designs are downloaded, which makes embroidery easy. Now, you can get a design in five minutes or less! The design is sent from the online dealer and e-mailed to you. Then, you can store the design somewhere on your computer.

To organize the designs on your computer, do the following:

1 | Go to start, My Computer, and double left click the icon for your C-drive.

2 | Right click on the desktop, and select New, Folder and type in Embroidery Designs.

3 | Keep the designs organized by category. I use flowers, sports, fonts, animals and baby. It is easy to find designs once you have taken the time to organize them. It is never too late to start organizing your designs. You can drag and drop your designs from wherever they are now to your new labeled folder.

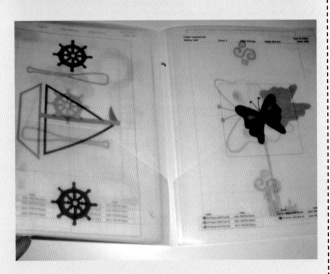

Save your designs periodically as well. Back them up on a CD, and store the CD in a safe place. This is especially important if you purchase a new computer.

Choosing Designs

By now, I am sure you have accumulated many designs in your machine format. The formats for most embroidery designs are: ART, DST, EXP, JEF, PES and SHV. When purchasing a design online, make sure you are buying the correct format. Online companies are not very forgiving with this type of mistake. Read the manual, and decide which format your machine uses. Always purchase designs from a reputable design company. It is tempting to buy from an auction-type seller, but beware because the quality can be terrible and the designs are copyrighted.

The designs included in this book are simple with few color changes. I like designs with only few color changes because it takes less time. Many designs with multiple color changes look absolutely wonderful, but overall, I think a design really should not have to have more than five colors. I can hear the embroidery designers screaming now! However, if you want to try something different, you can easily change the color changes in your embroidery software or at the machine. Try stitching the design first and then make any changes you like.

In most editing software, the stitch density can be adjusted. This is not necessary for any of the designs featured in this book, but as you become more familiar with machine embroidery, you may want to experiment. You may come across a design (usually a flower) with 15,000 stitches and 18 color changes. I would suggest decreasing the density of the design. Again, stitch a sample to make sure the change has not affected the overall look of the design. The fabric to be embroidered is an important factor to consider when you alter stitch density. Velour and terrycloth require a higher stitch count so the fabric will not show through.

Next, consider the scale of the design; it has to match the item to be embroidered. For example, small flowers look better on clothing or accessories than on a valance. Plan the project and adjust the design selection as needed. You can re-size most designs to a point, but there are limits. You couldn't re-size a ½-inch flower of 700 stitches to a 4-inch flower of 12,000 stitches and expect the same precise result. This step would have to be done with digitizing.

I confess — I do not digitize. Okay, my secret's out! I truly believe that with the quantity and quality of the thousands of designs available, it's not necessary for me to digitize. I do not enjoy the computer work as much as the creating and stitching, so I leave the digitizing up to the experts.

However, I do know how to manipulate a design. I enjoy mirror imaging, rotating, and copying and pasting designs. In this book, I merged designs together, but for the most part I did not change the designs for the projects. The few changes I did make to the designs could easily be done at your machine on the screen. In order to print a template for the project, you will need to edit it in software and print out the template.

If you already have a specific embroidery style, feel free to adapt the directions to fit your preferences. There are many ways of doing everything in life, so go ahead and experiment!

Embroidery Thread

There are many different types of thread that work wonderfully for embroidery. The primary choices are polyester, rayon and cotton.

Rayon thread has a shiny appearance that is caused by the tight twist in the manufacturing process. It is strong and durable but can't withstand bleaching.

Polyester thread is very strong and has a shiny appearance that is similar to rayon thread. It can be laundered with bleach and will not change color. It is especially useful for embroidering on towels, sheets and baby items because it can go through the wash.

Cotton thread is strong and has a natural feel to it. This type of thread would be used to achieve an antique look.

Most digitized designs are meant for 40-wt thread. I used only 40-wt. polyester thread for all of the projects in this book.

There are endless colors and brands of great embroidery thread. Thread is to embroiderers as fabric is to quilters. You will collect many spools of thread, and you will need them! Buy quality thread, and keep your thread stored in a handy box or on a wall rack. Wall racks are convenient because you can see at a glance exactly what you have while you are stitching.

Dust can collect on thread, and that is not good for your machine. Be sure to dust off the spools before threading your machine. Use a hair dryer, and blow quickly over the wall rack to remove the dust from the tops of the spools of thread.

Hooping Techniques

Follow these simple steps each time to hoop an item perfectly.

1 | Choose the correct size hoop for the project. Do not use a larger hoop than needed. The fabric has less a chance to pucker if you use a small hoop. Only when embroidering an appliqué design should you use a larger-size hoop. Using a larger hoop for the appliqué design makes trimming the fabric much easier to fit the scissors inside the hoop.

2 | Use shelf liner rubber matting on top of your work surface. Tape the mesh down with duct tape, and cut the rectangle larger than your largest embroidery hoop. This product helps to keep the hoop in place when hooping your fabric.

3 | Do not adjust the tension screw once your fabric has been hooped. This will cause puckering.

4 | Hoop the fabric and stabilizer, and test the fabric tension by pushing up from underneath the hoop. Make sure the fabric is as tight as a drum. If it is not, unhoop the fabric and tighten the screw. Rehoop the fabric.

5 | Check the fabric underneath: Turn the hoop over and make sure a collar or sleeve is not caught in between the hoop and stabilizer.

6 | Lay the template in the hoop to be certain the target sticker is still in the correct spot on the fabric. Begin stitching.

Materials Needed for Embroidery

Embroidery sewing machine, assorted hoops
Computer and printer
Embroidery editing software
Tracing paper trimmed to fit into printer
Stabilizers: cut-away, tear-away, sticky back and water soluble
Masking tape
Chalk
Temporary spray adhesive
Assorted embroidery blanks
Basic sewing notions

Embroidery needles and sewing needles
Scissors: embroidery curved scissors and pinking shears
Thread: embroidery and all purpose
Bobbins
Steam iron
Fusible interfacing
Therm O Web Heat'nBond
Fabric trims
Fabric
Target Stickers

airplanes!

Boys love airplanes, so send your little pilot on a flight of imagination with these fun, freewheeling designs. He will be ready for adventure in his miniature bomber jacket and overalls, and he can dream of flying through the clouds while cuddled under a fleecy white blanket. Decorate his room with a decorated director's chair, hamper, hat box and lamp, and you'll be ready for lift-off!

Chapter 2

Junior Pilot Overalls

Purchased boy's overalls are a perfect backdrop for small-scale embroidery designs. It is very difficult to actually find baby or toddler clothes that are not embellished in some way already. Many baby blankets, hooded towel sets and even strollers are color coded in "boy" or "girl" colors. When you find nice, unembellished blanks, stock up!

Remember to look for hoopability while you are shopping for blanks. Hoopability is a made-up word for embroiderers — you will understand the term once you have tried to hoop difficult items. Choose hoopable items that are easy to embroider. Do not make more work for yourself than necessary; after all, we want to enjoy our craft, not dread it!

Products Needed:

1 toddler-size denim overalls
Sticky-back stabilizer*
Target Stickers (contained in the Perfect
    Placement Kit)
Embroidery thread

On the CD:

Plane #1 and Plane #5 embroidery designs
Plane #1 and Plane #5 design templates

* Used in this project: Floriani Sticky-back stabilizer

Junior Pilot Overalls Instructions

1 | At the computer, open up the Plane #1 and Plane #5 designs and save them on a CD or memory card. Print out a template for each design on regular tracing paper. Usually you will need to trim the tracing paper to fit in your printer.

2 | Lay the template on the area you would like to highlight. In this case the pocket was easy to stick down and was the main focal point. It is totally acceptable to stitch right on the pocket, as this pocket will not be used by a small child and it is for decorative purposes. Place a target sticker in the exact center of the pocket. Use the template to determine if the design will fit. Pocket sizes may vary.

4 | Remove the hoop and tear away the sticky paper from the back of the overalls.

5 | Embroidering the center band is a bit more challenging. Lay the template of design Plane #1 on the center band. This design was a perfect fit, and no re-sizing was needed. I marked the two locations with Target Stickers and hooped the overalls the same way. The Perfect Placement Kit contains small, clear rulers that are a helpful tool for this project. I measured the distance from each belt loop. Use a structured piece of the garment as a base from which to measure. In this bottom photo, the belt loop was 40 mm from the center of the design on the target sticker.

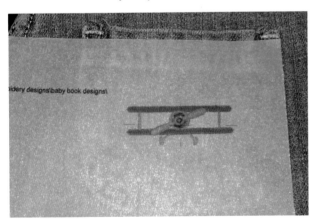

Template on pocket.

3 | Hoop a small hoop with the sticky-back stabilizer. Do not peel the protective paper off until after it is in the hoop. This can be done easily by scoring the paper with a pin. Place the overalls on the sticky paper. Do not remove your sticker until the needle is in the exact center of the design. Stitch design Plane # 5.

6 | Stitch one biplane and mirror image the biplane for the next design. I can mirror the image on my machine. If you can't, do it in your software and save it as a separate design.

7 | Remove the hoop and carefully tear away the stabilizer from the back of overalls.

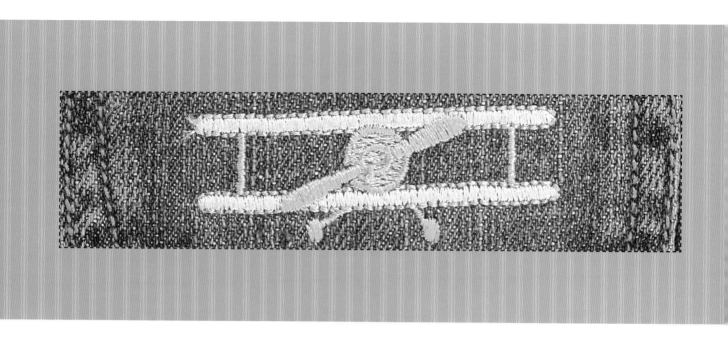

Satin-edged Blanket

Use a ready-made blank baby blanket, or sew one from soft fleece and add satin binding around the edges. I embroider a lot of baby blankets for my business, so I have a large stock of good-quality baby blankets. Use the appliqué airplane design in combination with your novelty fabrics to match the room décor. It's a great personalized and quick gift!

Products Needed:

1 fleece baby blanket (white)
Poly-mesh cut-away stabilizer*
Embroidery thread
Iron-on lightweight interfacing
½ yd. contrasting fabric
Curved embroidery scissors
Perfect Placement Kit (PPK) template for baby blankets
Target Stickers

On the CD:

Plane #3 Design template

*Used in this project: Floriani stabilizer

Satin-edged Blanket Instructions

1 | Save the Plane #3 design on a CD or memory card. Print out a template for Plane #3 on tracing paper. Lay the template marked "baby blanket" on one bottom corner of the blanket, and position the printed template of Plane #3 on top of that. You will use the top line on the PPK template. Line up the cross hairs on each and put a text Target Sticker underneath. The text Target Stickers are longer than the regular Target Sticker. Although we are not embroidering a line of text, the longer sticker helps you judge the position better. You can save time and do this step for the remaining three corners. Keep the Target Stickers in place while you hoop, and remove just before embroidering. This step guarantees the same placement for all four corners.

2 | Cut four 5"-square pieces of your contrasting fabric. Iron on the fusible interfacing to the wrong side of each square. Lay the template on top of the fabric to view exactly which features of the fabric will show through.

3 | Hoop the blanket with the poly mesh stabilizer in a medium-size hoop. The same steps will be used for all four corners.

4 | Check the placement of the design while in the hoop. Make sure the target sticker is in the correct spot. The first color of the design will be the outline of the entire design. This shows you where to place your fabric. When the stitching is complete, place the fabric square directly on that outline stitch. The next color will tack down the fabric.

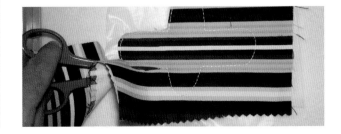

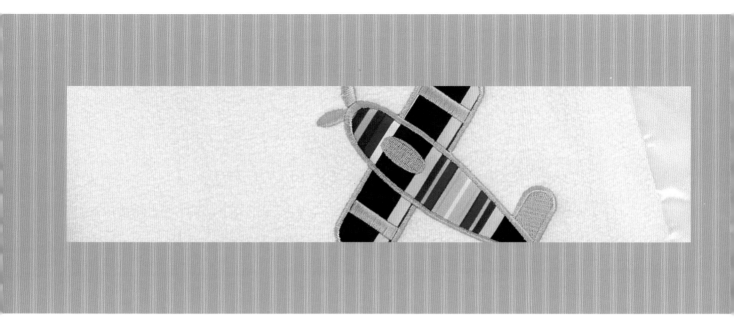

5 | Remove the hoop from the machine (but not the blanket from the hoop). Trim the excess fabric around the tack-down stitch as close as possible; you are practically trimming at the stitch line. Place the hoop back on the machine. Continue with the next color, which will be the satin stitch.

6 | After all four corners are stitched, trim the stabilizer from the blanket back.

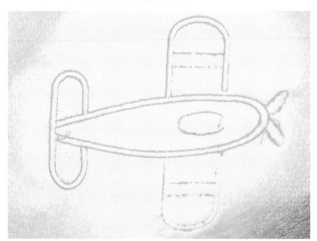

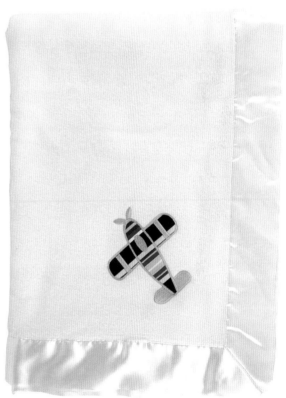

Design Tip:

Use the softest stabilizers available for baby clothing and accessories. Embroidery can feel uncomfortable next to a child's skin, so when embroidering directly on a garment that will touch the skin, iron a soft fusible interfacing on the back of the embroidery.

Director Chair

As embroiderers, we love to embellish anything we can. If we can hoop it, we will stitch it! One of the best features about the chair is the chair back canvas' hoopability. There is a small flap of fabric to cover the embroidery, and it is kept in place with hook-and-loop tape. This makes the back of the chair look clean and professional, and it also hides any leftover residue from the sticky paper.

This chair is a great practical gift for a nephew or godson. Look for these canvas seats online in blue or red. You can embroider these chairs for both boys and girls, adding different trims and designs to boost the ordinary colors.

Products Needed:

1 child's director chair in red
5" x 5" white fleece
12" decorative trim, cut in half
Curved embroidery scissors
Sticky-back tear-away stabilizer
Embroidery thread
Target Stickers

On the CD:

Plane #5 and Cloud embroidery designs
Plane #5 and Cloud design templates

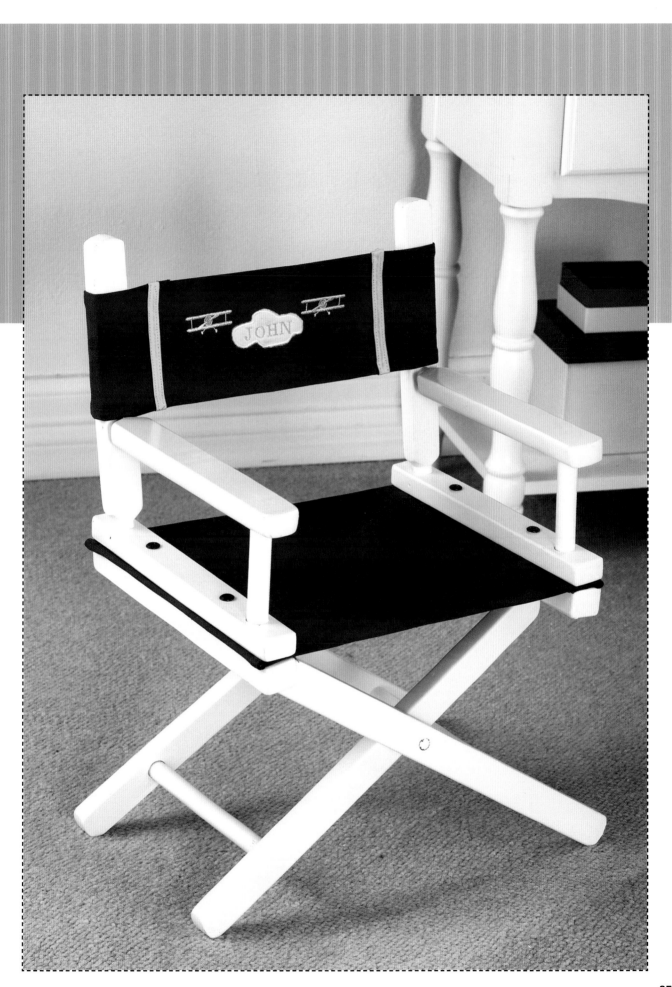

Director Chair Instructions

1 | Lay the templates of Plane #5 and Cloud embroidery designs on the chair back canvas (the small, rectangular piece of red canvas). There are 2 seams that run parallel to each other. Do not stitch past these seams, or you will not be able to fit the wood chair frame through the slots. Mark the design centers with a Target Sticker.

Design Tip:

I planned a symmetrical look with the two planes surrounding the appliquéd cloud.

2 | Hoop the sticky-back paper, but do not remove the protective paper until it is in the hoop. Score the paper with a pin, and remove the protective paper. This procedure keeps your hoop free of sticky residue. Lay the canvas on the hoop with Target Stickers still in place. Check the needle position before removing each target sticker.

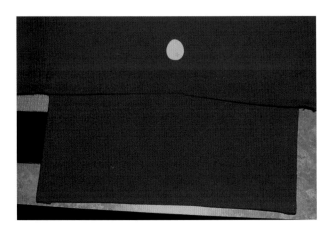

3 | Stitch the Cloud design first. An appliqué design is fairly simple to use when you have sharp scissors. The first color will mark the placement for your fabric. Lay the white fleece scrap on top of the stitch line. The next color will tack down the fleece fabric. After this step, trim the fleece as close to the stitching line as possible. Remove the hoop from the machine, but do not remove the fabric from the hoop. Lay the hoop on a flat surface and trim your fleece carefully. Replace the hoop, and finish with the satin stitch. The last color will be the satin stitch.

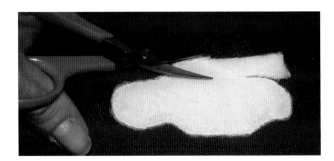

4 | Stitch the remaining two Plane #5 designs on both sides of the cloud. Check your target sticker placement, and embroider. You may also choose to personalize the chair with text; I added the name "John" to the inside of the appliquéd cloud. The font I used is a standard block programmed on my Baby Lock sewing machine.

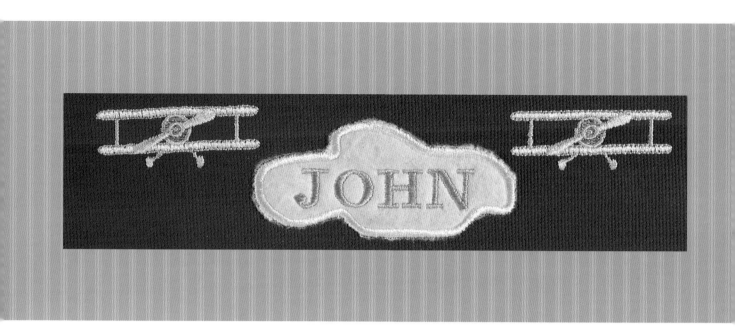

5 | Add the bias trim to both sides of the embroidery designs. The teal color was difficult to match, but this bias worked perfectly. Topstitch over the side seams, and tuck the raw ends under in back of chair.

Design Tip:

There are generally a few good, appropriate fonts that are easy to re-size at your machine — go ahead and use them! You will use your machine much more if you don't have to over-manipulate designs and text all of the time. There are so many options at your fingertips, and sometimes the choices are overwhelming. Simplify the layout and design of your embroidery, and you will enjoy it even more.

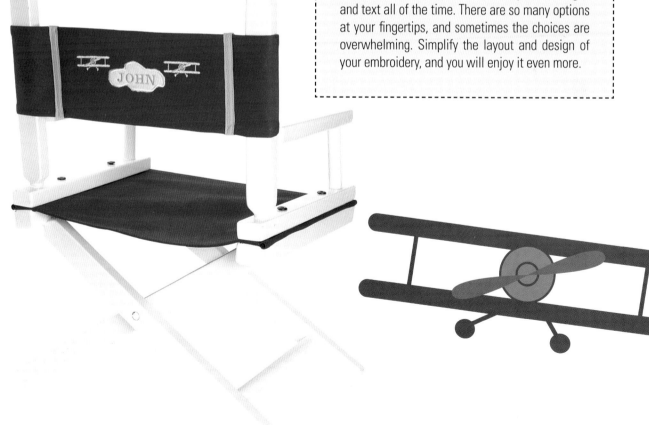

Up, Up and Away Hamper

There really is no end to the items we can embroider. Every time I visit a store, I am constantly looking for new blanks to embellish — and believe it or not, the laundry aisle is a great place to search. There are all kinds of canvas and collapsible fabric storage units sold just about everywhere. This canvas laundry hamper is large enough to be useful, and the fabric is wide enough to fit in my hoop. This particular hamper does not have to be hidden in the closet; you could also use it to store stuffed animals, blankets and pillows.

The lettering on the bag is a common font in my lettering software. I resized it to 50 mm, which is a bit large, but it was perfect for the large backdrop. When planning the whole design layout in your software, it is easy to merge all three separate designs into one large design. The two Plane #4 designs and the text (John) could also be saved separately and merged at your machine. If your machine does not have that capability, print out a separate template for each design and name to make sure that everything will fit perfectly.

Products Needed:

1 canvas hamper with wood frame
40" x 8" piece decorative fabric
Polyester embroidery thread (see CD for colors)
Medium-weight tear-away stabilizer
Target Stickers
Font for name (from your lettering software)

On the CD:

Plane #4 embroidery design
Plane #4 design template

Up, Up and Away Hamper Instructions

1 | Lay the canvas on your work surface and measure the width. Fold the sides together, and find the center of the bag. Next, measure how far down you would like to embroider. Mark this spot with a Target Sticker. Move the fabric strip down about 2" from the drawstring. Top-stitch the fabric strip around the entire bag, and press.

2 | Place the templates on the canvas bag underneath the fabric strip. Make sure that the designs are centered on the bag. Mark with Target Stickers for all three designs.

3 | Use your largest hoop, and place the tear-away stabilizer on the hoop with the canvas bag. Use the fabric strip as a guide to keep all of the embroidery perfectly horizontal and straight. Embroider the designs. When finished, remove the stabilizer.

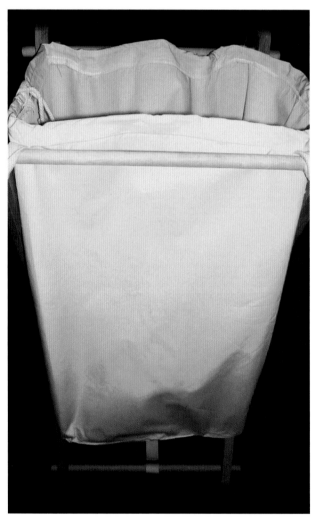

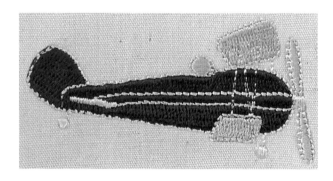

Flying Together Hat Box

This project takes patience and coordination (or an extra pair of hands!). Working with a round object on a flat surface can be difficult, but the end result is worth it.

Stackable hat boxes are sold in many craft stores, and they are available in a number of sizes. When purchasing a hat box, be sure it is heavy-weight cardboard. There is a flimsy alternative, but it will not hold up as well. Like many of my projects, the overall design of this hatbox emerged as I created it; I love the thrill of designing as I go! If you prefer, take the time to plan ahead and lay out your design.

Products Needed:

1 cardboard hatbox, 14" in diameter by 7½" tall
½ yd. decorative fabric for lid
45" x 8" solid fabric
Rick-rack trim (approximately 85" for 14"-diameter box)
Medium-weight fusible interfacing*
Iron-on adhesive*

Lightweight tear-away stabilizer*
Spray adhesive*
Stapler
Hot glue gun
Block lettering, 35 mm tall

*Used in this project: Baby Lock font, Pellon interfacing, Therm O Web Heat'nBond Iron-on Adhesive Ultra Hold, Floriani stabilizer, KK 2000

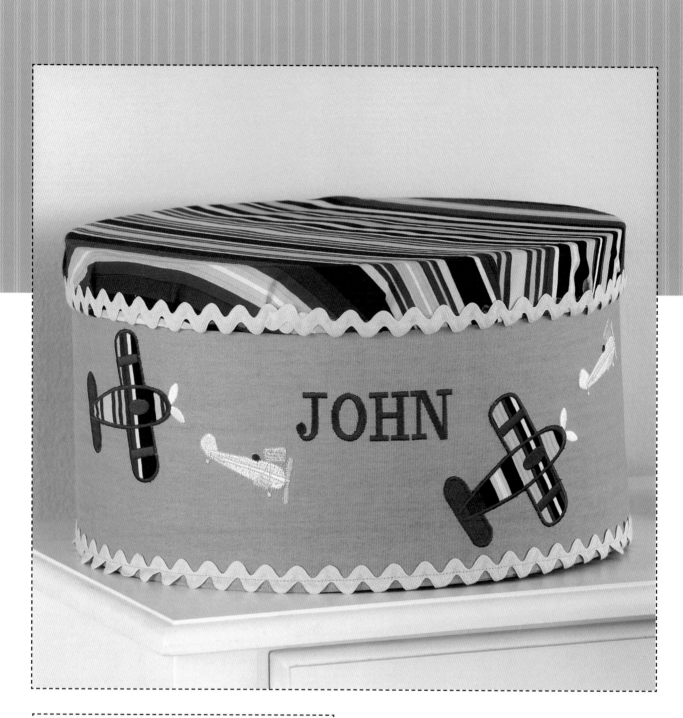

On the CD:

Plane #3 and Plane #4 embroidery designs

Flying Together Hat Box Instructions

1 | Iron the fusible interfacing on the wrong side of your solid piece of fabric. Fold edges under and stitch a ¼" seam on the top and bottom edges of the fabric. Lay the fabric on the hat box. Measure the drop of the lid (in this case, 1½"). Mark that measurement at the top of the hat box with a line of chalk. Do not embroider above this line, or the design could be chopped off once the lid is on the hatbox. Hoop the stabilizer with your fabric at one end.

Design Tip:

I like the idea of randomly placed airplanes. I wanted the scene to look as if the planes were chasing each other around the box. There are four groupings of the two planes and the name John centered between them all. The thread colors were chosen to match the fabric on the lid and the appliquéd airplane.

2 | Embroider the appliqué airplane and Plane #4. I find it easier to embroider the planes in groups of two. Rehoop each time. I left 4" between each set. I actually went back and added the name above the two sets of airplane designs for the center at the end.

3 | After you have finished all of the embroidery, sew the short end raw edge. I left one raw edge unsewn because it made the fabric too thick and the lid would not fit. Trial and error are sometimes a major turning point in the layout.

4 | Add the rick rack trim. Topstitch the trim on the bottom edge of the hat box.

5 | Position the striped fabric on top of the lid. Lightly spray the top of the lid with spray adhesive. Place the fabric on top, and press down. Turn the lid over, and staple the fabric to the edges of the lid. Fold the fabric a bit as you move along. Pull the fabric tightly, and staple as many times as needed to secure the fabric. After the fabric is stapled, hot glue the rick rack trim over the staples. Place a few dots of glue every couple of inches, and stick the trim to it.

6 | Iron the adhesive on the wrong side of the fabric, and then iron the fabric to the box, following manufacturer's instructions carefully. Ironing a round object is tricky. It works, but press down with the iron fairly hard and check for bubbles as you go. If you do have a few bubbles, re-iron and smooth out the fabric.

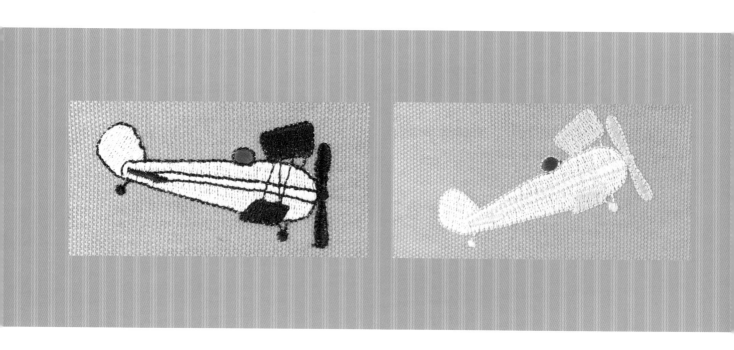

Bomber Jacket

One of my favorite places to search for blanks is at a resale shop or thrift store. These stores are perfect resources because their merchandise is unique and inexpensive. Why not buy a blank at a fraction of the retail cost? Sometimes you can find some very nice, high-quality items that are no longer sold in stores.

This child's denim jacket was three dollars at a local thrift store. As always, check all clothing very carefully. Examine the visible construction, such as snaps, buttons and zippers. Also, wash all items purchased from a thrift store before embroidering.

Products Needed:

1 child's denim jacket (plain back)
Medium-weight tear-away stabilizer*
Embroidery thread
Target Stickers
Chalk

On the CD:

Plane #3 and Plane #4 embroidery designs
Plane #3 and Plane #4 design templates

*Used in this project: Floriani stabilizer

Bomber Jacket Instructions

1 | Print templates of the Plane #3 and Plane #4 embroidery designs. Depending on the size of your jacket, two mirror-imaged Plane #4 designs should fit on the back yoke. Find the exact center of the back yoke of jacket, and mark the spot with chalk. Lay the templates on the upper back shoulder area, making sure that they are centered with the chalk mark. Mark the two locations with a Target Sticker.

2 | Hoop the jacket with medium-weight tear-away stabilizer in a hoop that will fit both designs side by side. If you do not have a large enough hoop, or if the jacket is too small, rehoop the jacket for each design. Leave all Target Stickers in place just until you are ready to stitch.

3 | Move down the center of the jacket to the middle back. Mark the center of the Plane #3 design with a Target Sticker. Embroider the design as an outline stitch without the appliqué.

4 | After embroidering, draw the spiraling lines coming from the end of the plane with chalk. Use a stitch that has three parallel lines (called the triple stretch stitch) to sew twirling lines in matching thread.

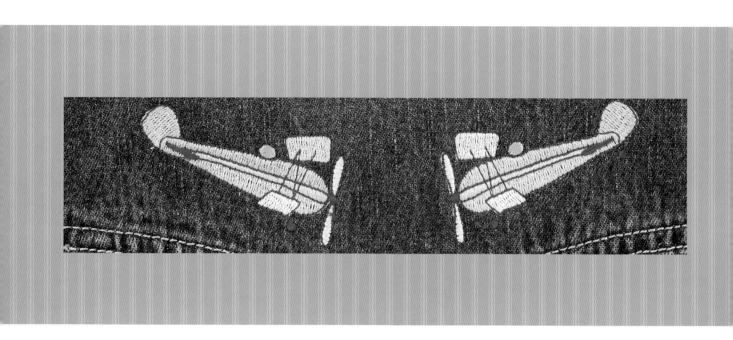

Design Tip:

This design is the appliqué airplane, and you can embroider it without the fabric — just delete the tack-down stitch and move ahead to the satin stitch. Be sure to use contrasting thread to make the design more noticeable.

Lift-off Lampshade

I had always wanted to sew fabric on a lampshade, and this book gave me the perfect opportunity. There are endless possibilities for embroidering lampshades. Use airplanes and primary colors for a little boy's room, or try different color combinations and designs for a teenager or college student.

This purchased lampshade has a sticky surface and is available in many sizes and shapes. Choose the shade that you will embroider, and decide which particular design layout you prefer. Make sure that the shade is a bit bigger than the lamp base so it will fit proportionately.

Products Needed:

1 sticky-surface lampshade (available at craft stores or
    online)
1"-wide red bias tape
¼ yd. red cotton fabric
Block-style font*
Two fabric scraps of contrasting fabric
Lightweight tear-away stabilizer*
Embroidery thread
Target Stickers
Chalk or non-marking pen
Pinking shears

On the CD:

Plane #3 embroidery design
Plane #3 template

*Used in this project: Baby Lock font, Floriani stabilizer

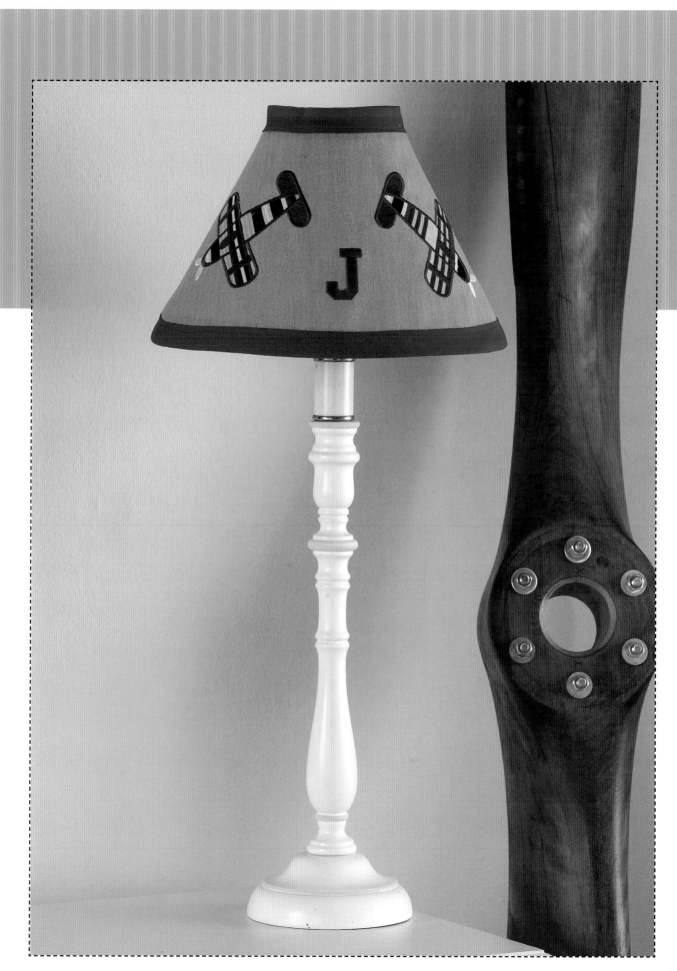

Lift-off Lampshade Instructions

1 | Remove the protective paper from the lampshade surface. The paper will be used as a template for your fabric. Lay the paper on your fabric, and trace around it with chalk or non-marking pen, following the manufacturer's instructions printed on the lampshade. Do not cut the fabric yet. It is always easier to hoop a larger piece of fabric than to try to fit your designs into a small piece of fabric.

2 | Lay the Plane #3 design template on the red fabric. Try to keep the designs close together, centered in the middle of the shade. Mark your exact center spot with a Target Sticker, and mark the two locations for the planes as well. Leave room for the initial to be embroidered. You probably don't need a template, but if you prefer to use one, print one out.

3 | Your entire piece of fabric should fit in a large-size hoop, so re-hooping is not necessary. Stitch out all three designs, two Plane #3 designs and one initial. Carefully remove the stabilizer from the back of the fabric. Cut away the extra fabric by following the lines you have traced from the template. Use pinking shears so the fabric does not fray.

4 | Cut two pieces of the bias trim, and topstitch them to the raw edges of the red fabric at the top and bottom. Leave about ½" at the ends to overlap at the seam.

5 | Lay the red fabric on the sticky surface, line up all the edges, and smooth as you go. You may need to reposition the fabric a few times to make it smooth. After the fabric is smooth, overlap the back seam and connect it with a dot of hot glue.

Design Tips:

You will usually only see the front of the shade, so place most of the embroidery on the front.

I embroidered a large block-style "J" in red thread in the center between the two airplane designs. Embroidering a name or initial personalizes the project a bit more.

flower garden

Decorate your little girl's room in flowers to make her feel sweet and precious all year long. Shower her with blossoms in a lovely decorated sweatsuit, and place an embroidered ribbon on her favorite teddy bear. Store her things in an adorned hatbox and basket, and make her room beautiful with a dainty, embroidered lampshade. Any little girl will love these projects!

Chapter 3

Blossom Sweatsuit

A purchased sweat suit is easy to embellish with embroidery. Children's clothing is usually very challenging to embroider, but this jacket worked well because it had a front zipper. You can easily place one side of the jacket on sticky paper on your hoop and embroider one side at a time. The matching pants are another story. The designs were too large to fit at the bottom hem area, so I decided to tie the outfit together with the coordinating trim.

The decorative trim was machine sewn to the bottom of the leggings and the jacket bottom hem edge. Wash the trim first in cold water to make sure it will not bleed on the finished garment. The trim pulls together all the colors of the embroidery without overpowering the jacket. I found this trim in my stash, and it turned out to be the perfect color combination to match the variegated thread.

Products Needed:

1 girl's sweatsuit outfit
Embroidery thread
Fusible poly-mesh stabilizer
Lightweight tear-away stabilizer
Water-soluble stabilizer
1½ yd. decorative ribbon trim
Target Stickers

On the CD:

Flower #2, Flower #3 and Flower #4 embroidery designs
Flower #2, Flower #3 and Flower #4 design templates

Blossom Sweatsuit Instructions

1 | Iron the fusible stabilizer to the two front sides of the jacket.

2 | Lay the Flower #2 and Flower #3 design templates on your garment. Position the templates as you like, or as they fit. Mark the design center with a Target Sticker for each location. Take into consideration pockets, zippers and seams. You will be working on a small area, so it is important to plan ahead and use templates. Use your best judgment to place the designs in an attractive arrangement.

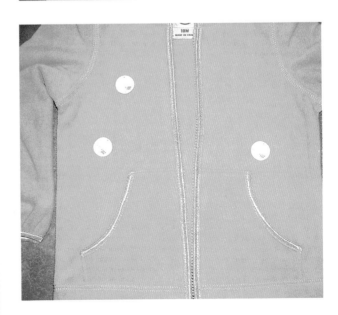

Design Tip:

Try to keep designs natural-looking. Don't be too focused on symmetry — use groups of three designs, rather than two or four, for an organic feel.

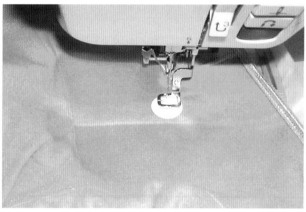

3 | Stitch the Flower #4 design to the opposite side of the jacket. When all embroidery is finished, remove your jacket from the sticky paper. The poly-mesh stabilizer will keep the jacket from losing its shape. Remove carefully.

4 | Lay out the trim according to the jacket design. Topstitch the decorative trim to the pant leg bottoms, jacket hem and cuffs. Be careful when sewing around any features such as zippers or buttons. Press with a warm iron when you are finished sewing.

Design Tip:

Adding decorative ribbon trim ties the designs and colors together; otherwise, the pants would look plain and unfinished. Make sure that you wash the ribbon in cold water to test its color fastness before sewing it to embroidered clothing.

Blooming Burp Cloths

This project is very quick and easy. Blank burp cloths (these started out as cloth diapers) are wonderful for embellishing to coordinate with the room theme. Make a basketful of burp cloths, one for each day of the week. Embroider a different design, and add matching trim to each one. Place the burp cloths in an embroidered, lined basket and you have an "over-the-top" baby shower gift that the expecting mother will love.

There are several different types of burp cloths. I prefer heavyweight all-cotton burp cloths; you can find them at large retailers and online.

Products Needed:

2 blank heavyweight all-cotton burp cloths
¼ yd. ostrich trim
¼ yd. pleated ribbon
Lightweight tear-away stabilizer
Perfect Placement Kit template for burp cloths
Target Stickers

On the CD:

Flower #3 and Flower #4 embroidery designs

Blooming Burp Cloth Instructions

1 | Lay the burp cloth on your work surface and center a template on top of the cloth. Mark the center with a Target Sticker. Repeat this step for both burp cloths. Embroider one design on each cloth, and remove the stabilizer from the back.

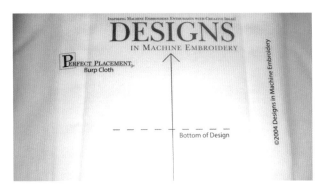

2 | Sew the decorative trim the bottom of each burp cloth. Match the thread color to your trim color (I add 2" on each end to wrap around the back of the burp cloth). Choose a trim that can be washed and dried easily.

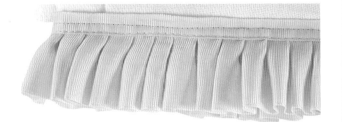

3 | After sewing the trim, press each burp cloth.

Lovely Lined Basket

There are many fabric-lined baskets available in a wide variety of colors. I generally use them to hold hard-to-wrap gifts, such as towel sets, robes or stuffed animals. When you are shopping for a good basket with a liner, make sure the liner comes down over the basket at least two inches. Remember, you can add trim to these as well as embroidery. I am constantly looking for easy ways to jazz up or embellish a blank product.

Products Needed:

1 lined basket
Lightweight tear-away stabilizer
Embroidery thread
Target Stickers
Masking tape
Hot glue gun and glue (optional)

On the CD:

Flower #3 and Flower #4 embroidery designs
Flower #3 and Flower #4 design templates

Lovely Lined Basket Instructions

1 | Choose the area of the basket that you want to embroider. I chose the center front area because this basket has a nice square shape. Mark the top edge of the liner with masking tape. Do not embroider past this edge, because you will not see the embroidery on the inside of the basket. Mark the center of the liner with a Target Sticker (it is easiest to do this while the liner is still in the basket). Remove the liner and lay the template of your design on the Target Sticker. Check to make sure that the design fits and will not overlap the edge line. If you are sure the design will fit, hoop the liner with the stabilizer. If the design is too large, re-size it in your software to make it smaller.

Design Tip:

You will not see the back of the basket if it is sitting on a shelf or in a bookcase — so if the back will not show, you may not need to embroider all the way around the basket.

2 | Embroider the designs on the fabric liner. Choose thread colors that will match with the room or the gift you are putting in the basket. Do not forget to coordinate your trim or ribbon with the embroidery designs.

3 | Remove the stabilizer from the back of the fabric liner. Add the ribbon and tie in a bow. Adding the ribbon was very easy, because the liner actually had loops sewn at the bottom. If your liner has no loops, you can use a few dabs of hot glue to hold the ribbon in place around the basket.

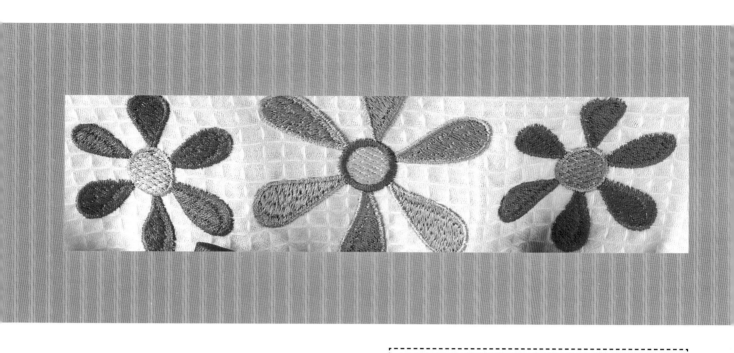

Design Tip:

Instead of tying a ribbon around the basket, try sewing another type of trim at the bottom.

Flowered, Fringed Lampshade

I enjoyed making the pilot lampshade so much that I decided to try it again with the flowers. Doing this project a second time was much easier and quicker, naturally. For this lampshade, I wanted to design a more feminine and fun look, so the decorative trims came into play. I love ostrich and eyelash trim. They give my diverse items great texture and color. This project would look completely different without the trim.

Products Needed:

1 sticky-surface square lampshade
½ yd. hot pink cotton duck fabric
1 yd. hot pink ostrich trim
2 8" x 2" strips contrasting fabric (striped fabric)
1 scrap striped fabric for appliqué
Tear-away stabilizer
Embroidery thread
Target Stickers
Chalk or non-marking pen
Hot glue gun and hot glue

On the CD:

Flower #3, Flower #4 and Flower #5 embroidery designs
3 Flower #5 design templates

Flowered, Fringed Lampshade Instructions

1 | Remove the protective paper from the lampshade, and lay it on the right side of the pink fabric. Trace the lampshade shape on the pink fabric with chalk or a non-marking pen. Do not cut your fabric.

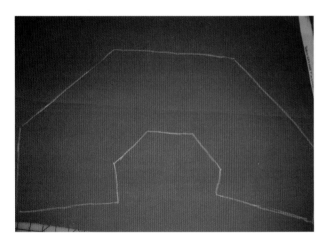

2 | To break up the lampshade into thirds, I topstitched two strips of the striped fabric. The position of the strips was determined by the sections of the shade. This shade was square, so I sewed the strips on the two front angles. To sew the strips, fold the raw edges under and press with an iron. Topstitch them in place, and leave about ½" of the raw edge at the bottom. You will trim all of it away later and it will be covered with the trim.

3 | After the strips are sewn, lay your Flower #5 design templates on the fabric. If your size shade permits, use this design three times in a row. Mark each Flower #5 center with a Target Sticker. I used the center flower as an appliqué and the flowers on either side embroidered in the satin outline stitch. I used the same color at all color stops. Embroider the three designs.

4 | Remove stabilizer from back of fabric carefully. You can cut the fabric along the chalk line with pinking shears.

5 | Topstitch the lime ostrich trim at the top and bottom edges of the shade. Bump the seam edges together, and touch with a dot of hot glue on the back if needed.

Design Tip:

If the lampshade will be viewed from all angles, you can easily sew one back edge seam with a straight stitch. This will give the back seam a more finished look. Add about one inch to your template edge — one seam will overlap the other.

Easy Organza Ribbon

One of my favorite things to embroider is wired ribbon. Most people can't believe how easy it is! Wired ribbon is everywhere, in every imaginable color. The wire actually helps keep the ribbon taut in the hoop, so there is no need for sticky-back stabilizers. Believe me, it works!

You can embroider on ribbon for all kinds of gifts. Give a large teddy bear with an embroidered ribbon to a new baby — embroider the ribbon on one side with the baby's name, and on the other with the birth date. It is a beautiful, quick and thoughtful gift. After all embroidery is complete, you can gently remove the wire from the ribbon. Just pull slightly on the wire and it will come out.

Products Needed:

1½ yd. 2"-wide wired ribbon
Water-soluble stabilizer
Embroidery thread
Masking tape

On the CD:

Flower #3 embroidery design

Easy Organza Ribbon Instructions

1 | You must first determine the length of the ribbon needed for a large-size bow to fit around the teddy bear. Any size bear will work, but a 12" or larger size bear looks nice. Before I cut the ribbon, I wrap it around the bear and tie it in a bow. Mark the two end sections from under the bow on the tail end edges with masking tape. This is the only area that will be embroidered.

2 | Hoop the two tail ends with the water-soluble stabilizer. The ends will be parallel to each other in the hoop. Make sure you are not embroidering above the masking tape line.

3 | I embroidered three designs of Flower #3, changing the color sequence but using the same colors. After both tail ends are embroidered, remove the ribbon from the hoop. Carefully remove the ribbon from the stabilizer. You do not have to wet the stabilizer. Gently remove the wire from the end of the ribbon by pulling the wire from the bottom of each side.

Design Tip:

If the ribbon is purely for decorative purposes, then you may leave the wire in the ribbon. Wired ribbon makes an easy bow when tied.

Beautiful Bath Towel Set

One great accessory to any room or bath is coordinating towels. Embroidering on a fabric panel eliminates the trouble of embroidering thick towels. Use an iron-on fusible interfacing to give more stability to the fabric, and add a matching rick-rack trim to the edges of the panel to pull it all together. Most towel sets are very thick and plush, which makes for a beautiful personalized towel; however, they can be difficult to embroider. If you have trouble embroidering towels, remember two things: use appropriate design selections, and stitch the design twice if you are not satisfied with the stitch coverage. Choose designs that aren't too small or intricate. Stitch the design or monogram twice if you are in doubt about the quality. Keep the hoop in the machine and hit start again after the first time has completed.

Products Needed:

2 terrycloth hand towels
1 bath towel
Medium-weight tear-away stabilizer
Coordinating fabric strips to cover the border on each towel (approximately 4" x 20")
Pink fabric scraps for flower applique
Medium-weight iron-on fusible interfacing
4 yd. light pink rick-rack trim
2 yd. white rick-rack trim
Target Stickers
Curved embroidery scissors

On the CD:

Flower #1, Flower #3 and Flower #5 embroidery designs
Flower #1, Flower #3 and Flower #5 design templates

Beautiful Bath Towel Set Instructions

1 | Iron on the fusible interfacing to the wrong side of two fabric panel sections for the hand towels, and one section for the bath towel.

2 | At the computer, open up the Flower #1 and Flower #3 designs in your editing software. I merged the designs together and saved it as a new design, Towel 1. Print a template of design Towel 1. Print a template of Flower #5.

3 | Hoop one hand towel fabric panel with the medium-weight tear-away stabilizer. Embroider the design renamed Towel 1 on both hand towels. Remove stabilizer from back of fabric.

4 | Take the bath towel fabric panel (striped fabric), and lay the Flower #5 template on top. Mark the three locations for embroidery with Target Stickers. Hoop this fabric panel in a large hoop. Use a larger hoop than the design calls for, if possible, when stitching an appliqué; it makes cutting away the extra fabric between colors much easier.

5 | Stitch appliqué Flower #5, and trim all fabric as needed between color stops. I used lime green thread for all colors in the appliqué.

6 | Trim all edges of the fabric panels with pinking shears.

7 | Fold under raw edges of bath towel panel and topstitch in place. Press with an iron.

8 | Stitch the rick-rack trim on both hand towels.

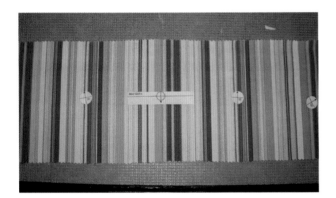

Summery Stripes Hat Box

Here is another take on the cardboard hat box. The hat boxes are actually a group of four stackable boxes made of very sturdy cardboard. When purchasing this type of hat box, be certain it is made of sturdy cardboard. You will be pressing down fairly hard to iron on the fabric and you would not want to crush the box. This is a fun project that can be finished many ways. It can be a creative and practical addition to a nursery or toddler's room. Use some interesting coordinating fabrics and trim to make a one-of-a-kind decoration. Remember not to use a super-thick fabric. Using thick fabric will make it difficult to fit the lid closed. I did not line the hat boxes, but you can easily do that. Cut your lining fabric by using the box as a template, and use spray adhesive on the fabric. Cut one long piece for the sides and a circle for the bottom of the box.

Products Needed:

1 heavyweight cardboard hat box
½ yd. yellow cotton duck fabric
(4) 6" x 3½" strips striped fabric
Striped fabric for top of lid (size depends on lid
    measurement)
½ yd. hot pink ostrich fringe
½ yd. hot pink rick-rack trim
Medium-weight fusible interfacing*

Iron-on adhesive*
Lightweight tear-away stabilizer*
Chalk
Spray adhesive*
Stapler
Hot glue gun

*Used in this project: Pellon Interfacing, Therm O Web Heat'nBond Iron-on Adhesive Ultra Hold, Floriani stabilizer, KK 2000 spray adhesive

On the CD:

Flower #3 and Flower #4 embroidery designs
Flower #3 and Flower #4 design templates

Summery Stripes Hat Box Instructions

1 | Iron on the fusible interfacing on the wrong side of your solid piece of fabric. Stitch a ¼" seam on the top and bottom edges of the fabric. Lay the fabric on the hat box. Measure the drop of the lid; this lid drop measured 1½". Mark this measurement at the top of the hat box with a line of chalk. This step is done so you do not embroider too close to the top where it will not be seen under the lid. A design could also be chopped off once the lid is placed on top. Fold the fabric in half vertically and place a Target Sticker in that spot. This will be your center of the hat box. This hat box has three sections of embroidery.

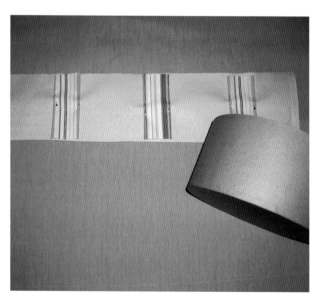

2 | Hoop the light-weight tear-away stabilizer with the yellow fabric. Embroider Flower #4 in center. Remove fabric from hoop and stabilizer from back. Topstitch striped fabric strips to either side of Flower #4.

3 | Lay the Flower #3 templates on the yellow fabric. You will embroider two designs of Flower #3 in the segments between the striped fabric strips. Mark the location for each Flower #3 with a Target Sticker. After embroidering the Flower #3 designs, topstitch the remaining fabric strips on opposite ends of the two sets of flowers.

4 | Remove the stabilizer from the back of the yellow fabric.

5 | Position the striped fabric on top of the lid. Lightly spray the top of the lid with spray adhesive. Stick the fabric on top and press down. Turn the lid over and staple the fabric to the edges of the lid. Fold the fabric a bit as you move along. Pull the fabric tightly and staple as many times as needed. You will cover the staples with trim, so don't worry if the staples don't look neat.

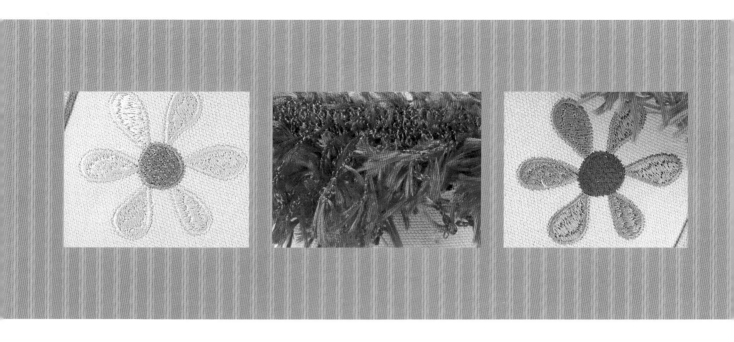

6 | After the fabric is stapled, hot glue the ostrich trim over the staples. Place a few dots of glue every few inches and stick the trim to it. Adding the rick-rack trim was by far the easiest part of the project. Topstitch the trim on the bottom edge of the hat box fabric.

7 | Iron the iron-on adhesive to the wrong side of the fabric. Follow the directions for applying this exactly as stated. It worked wonderfully for this project, but I went step by step as they recommended. The technique actually adheres the fabric to the box when ironed. This is the tricky part — ironing a round object. It works, but press down with the iron fairly hard and check for bubbles as you go. I did have a few bubbles, but I was able to re-iron and smooth out the fabric.

nautical nursery

These nautical-themed designs will grow with your child, and they are perfect for a baby's room. With some small adjustments to bedding and accessories, sailboats and anchors will still be appropriate when the baby grows up. I grew up at the seashore, and I always think of returning for vacations.

By keeping the embroidery design simple, it is easy to use many color variations and fabric patterns. The navy blue and bold yellow color pallet complement each other and make the designs really pop. These classic color combinations will always work together.

Chapter 4

Coastal Crib Bumpers

When you think of a crib and the bedding that will go into it, you have to remember the baby's view. A baby does not see out of the crib for a long time. Make the crib bumpers interesting, and give your baby something to look at. The sailboat design is simple and the embroidery is large. The appliqué designs really speed up the embroidery process. The most important item to remember is to keep all of the embroidery straight. Also, consider whether you would like to embroider on both sides of the bumper. The crib will generally be placed along one or two sides of a wall, so you may not need to embroider on those sides.

Products Needed:

Crib bumper pattern and pattern supplies*
¼ yd. contrasting fabric for appliqué designs
Crib bumper pre-cut foam
2 yd. grosgrain ribbon
½ yd. sew-in hook-and-loop tape
Medium-weight tear-away stabilizer
Medium-weight iron-on fusible interfacing
Polyester embroidery thread
Spray adhesive
Tracing paper (trim to fit printer)
Target Stickers

On the CD:

Boat #1 and Nautical Wheel embroidery designs

*Used in this project: Simplicity Pattern #4627 Nursery Accessories

Coastal Crib Bumpers Instructions

1 | Open up the Boat #1 and Nautical Wheel embroidery designs in your editing software. Combine the Boat #1 and two Nautical Wheel designs to either side of the sailboat. Save this new design as Boat 3. Print a template of Boat 3 on tracing paper. You will use this template for your layout.

2 | Cut the light-blue fabric for bumpers, and follow the pattern directions for construction after all embroidery is complete.

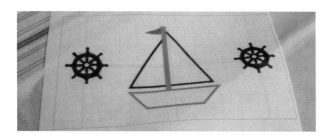

3 | Take two long sides of the bumpers, and fold them in half horizontally. Press. This pressed line will be your guide for all embroidery designs to "sit" on. A straight line reference is helpful when embroidering on long, blank backgrounds, and this technique is great for embroidering on a top sheet border or valance. Place the template of the Boat #3 (one sailboat with two wheels at each side of sailboat). Mark the center of the bumper fabric with a Target Sticker. Embroider the Boat 3 design in three separate sets, with three hoopings. Start in the middle and continue with the remaining two sets.

4 | Take the fabric that will be used for appliqué, in this case the yellow with blue dots, and iron on the fusible interfacing. This step will give the appliqué more stability and also keep the fabric from fraying. It is easier and makes a large project move along more quickly when you do these particular steps are taken ahead of time. If you are interrupted in the middle of embroidery (this happens to all of us), you can easily jump back where you left off.

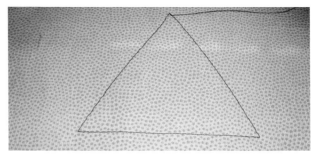

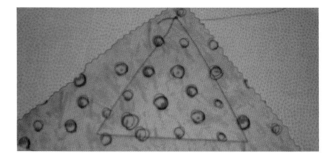

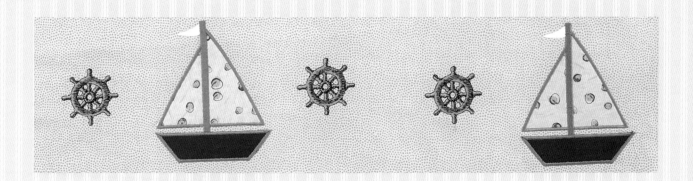

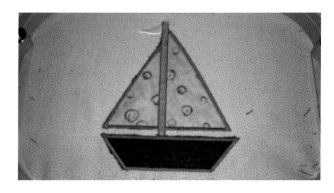

5 | After all embroidery is finished, complete the short end bumpers. The embroidery is the same layout, but I switched the fabric. Yellow/blue dot fabric for background and light blue for appliqué. Fold the fabric horizontal and use templates for exact design location. Mark with a target sticker for the center. Iron on the fusible interfacing on the light blue fabric (only needed for two designs).

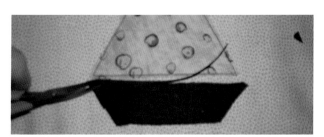

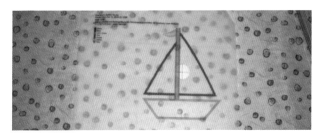

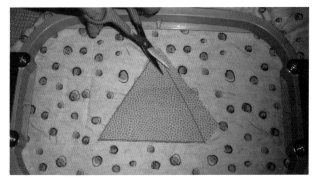

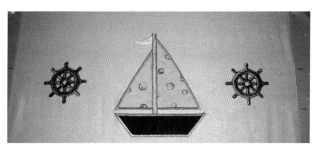

6 | Follow the pattern directions for constructing the bumpers. You may want to sew Velcro at each bumper end for laundering purposes. Sew the middle and ends of each bumper with matching grosgrain ribbon, tie around crib rails. Please follow safety standards when sewing and decorating for babies. Crib bumpers should fit snugly; double-knot all ties that will be reachable.

Seashore Organizer

We know babies require a lot of work. We also know babies require a lot of stuff. This fabric organizer is a great item to keep in a nursery or at grandma's house. You can fill it with powder, lotions and wipes. You can even add Velcro to the ends to make it easier to reposition and relocate. I suggest making pockets wider as opposed to deeper. This is a good tip for most items with pockets. Pockets that are too deep (long) tend to lose things. Make the pockets a bit wider, or make more pockets. By changing the pattern a bit, I was able to make the straps out of cotton webbing instead of ribbon and added another row of pockets.

Products Needed:

Organizer pattern and required fabrics/supplies*
Fusible fleece batting
1 yd. 1"-wide white cotton webbing
10" white hook-and-loop tape*
Medium-weight tear-away stabilizer
Fusible interfacing
¼ yd. yellow/blue fabric
1 yd. blue/white stripe fabric
Embroidery thread
Target Stickers

On the CD:

Boat #1 and Anchor embroidery designs
Boat #1 and Anchor design templates

*Used in this project: Velcro, Simplicity pattern #4627

Seashore Organizer Instructions

1 | Cut out fabric for the organizer and add 7" to the length for an extra pocket. You can easily change this step if you prefer one row of pockets. You will need to add 5½" for an additional pocket. All embroidery will take place before construction of pockets to base of organizer. The yellow/blue dot fabric was also added at the top of each row of pockets. This step is very easy and really adds a finished and tailored look to the top edges. The strips are 3" long and as wide as pocket sections. Fold the yellow strips in half horizontally and press with an iron. Stitch the raw edges of yellow fabric along the raw edges of top pocket. Fold over the yellow fabric to inside the pocket and topstitch in the ditch. This is an easy and quick way to finish many items (quilts, edges of towels, etc.). Continue for both rows of pockets.

2 | Lay the pocket pieces on a flat surface and position the templates as shown in photo. The top row of pockets has four anchors embroidered in a straight line. Use a Target Sticker to mark the design location for each spot. Hoop the tear-away stabilizer and embroider all four anchors.

3 | Iron the fusible interfacing to the yellow/blue fabric for appliqué. Fold pocket piece in half lengthwise and mark the center with a Target Sticker. This will be the location for the appliqué sailboat design.

4 | Follow directions for organizer assembly. Take into consideration the embroidery designs on the pockets. You do not want to stitch over the embroidery.

5 | Add the webbing strips at the top, and sew hook-and-loop tape to each end for attachment.

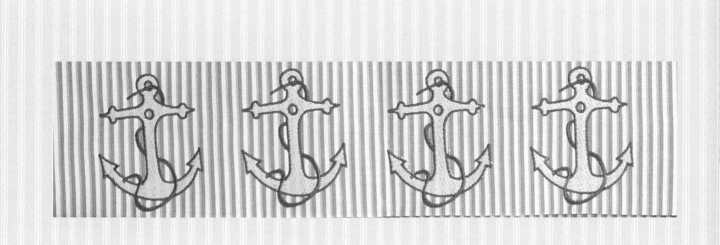

Ahoy! Crib Skirt

This crib skirt is one of the easiest projects in the book. Purchase a navy blue crib skirt from a retail store, or make your own from a pattern. Then, decide on the embroidery placement. Will the crib be against the wall or two walls? Again, you don't have to embroider on sides that will not show. The skirt is gathered, which can cause some embroidery difficulty, but if you keep the embroidery simple, the designs will not get lost in gathered pleats. The paddle design is perfect for a simple outline, or you could use it as an appliqué design.

Products Needed:

1 navy blue crib skirt
Lightweight tear-away stabilizer
Embroidery thread
Target Stickers

On the CD:

Lifesaver and Paddle embroidery designs

Ahoy! Crib Skirt Instructions

1 | Open the Lifesaver and Paddle embroidery designs in your embroidery editing software. Copy and paste or merge the Paddle design above the Lifesaver design. Save the new design as Lifesaver 2 (the designs are not resized). Print out two templates of the new design.

2 | Fold the crib skirt in half, matching each long side seam or opening for slats. Work from the center outward. Lay a template of Lifesaver 2 in the middle of the crib skirt: mark the location with a Target Sticker. Measure 7" between designs; there should be five groups of design Lifesaver 2. You will need to re-hoop five times for each long side of the crib skirt. Three groups of designs fit well on the two short ends of the crib skirt. Follow the same directions for the short sides.

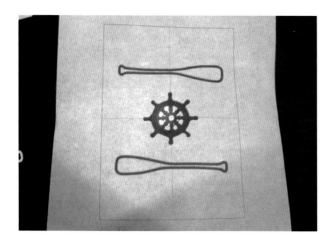

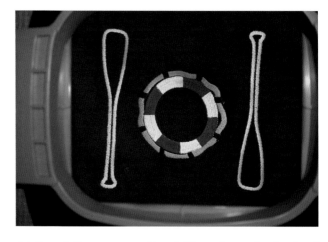

3 | Carefully remove all stabilizer from the back of crib skirt, and trim threads.

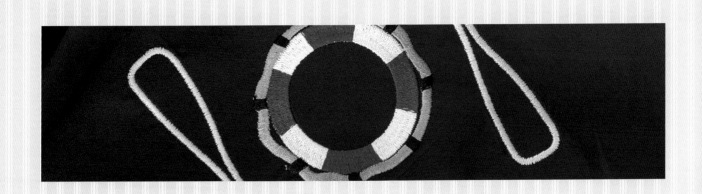

Design Tips:

Use bright contrasting colors when embroidering on dark fabrics.

Choose a design with four or fewer colors to make the embroidery process move much faster. Look ahead at the color chart when selecting designs to determine whether some colors can be deleted.

Ocean Waves Valance

This lovely, tailored valance is an excellent example of trim embellishment. I designed this valance to enhance the total natural look of the nursery. Large rick-rack trim is the perfect touch for the embroidered valance. Think about practical elements while you are planning the overall design, such as the width of the window and what type of coverage you need. You can also line the valance if you like. The rod pocket is approximately three inches long. Sew it by folding over the top portion of the navy blue fabric and creating a pocket in the back. Although this project takes a bit more time, it's worth it!

Break up the large, blank canvas by sewing yellow/blue dot fabric and light blue fabric in a border. The fabrics are different weights: navy-blue cotton duck, light-blue and yellow/blue dot are both lightweight cotton twills. To equalize them, iron a lightweight fusible interfacing on the wrong side of each of the light cotton fabrics.

Products Needed:

Navy blue cotton duck fabric, size determined by
   window width (add 5" for return of valance and
   ½" seam allowance)
¼ yd. yellow/blue dot fabric
¼ yd. light blue fabric
2½ yd. large white rick-rack trim
Target Stickers
Embroidery thread
Medium-weight fusible interfacing

On the CD:

Boat #1, Anchor and Nautical Wheel embroidery
   designs
3 Boat #1 design templates

Valance measures 20" from top to bottom edge.

Ocean Waves Valance Instructions

1 | Open Nautical Wheel and Anchor embroidery designs in your embroidery software, and copy and paste the Anchor with two Nautical Wheel designs. Save this new design as Anchor 2. Print a template of the Anchor 2 design on tracing paper. You can re-use the template of design Boat #1. Print two more.

2 | Iron the fusible interfacing to the border fabrics.

3 | Press the yellow/blue dot fabric under ½" on both long sides. Topstitch the yellow/blue dot fabric 3" below the top edge of the valance. You will be stitching in the ditch of the rod pocket seam for the top seam.

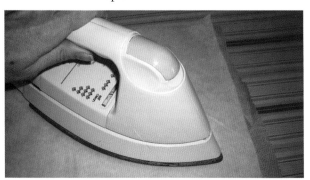

4 | Fold the light blue fabric in half lengthwise, and mark the center with a target sticker. Lay the Anchor template and three Boat #1 templates on the light blue fabric. Mark each design placement with a target sticker. The blue fabric will be embroidered and then sewn on the navy blue fabric edge. The amount of design groups embroidered depends on the width of your window. This valance has three groups of the Anchor 2 design and six Boat #1 designs. Embroider the center design first then the remaining designs.

5 | Remove stabilizer from back of fabric. Sew the light blue fabric on top of the navy blue fabric at the bottom edge. The raw edges will be covered with the rick-rack trim.

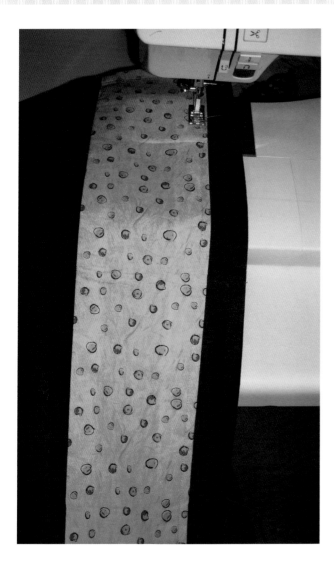

The white rick-rack covers the raw edge at the bottom of the valance.

Press the raw edges of each side seam under ½", and topstitch with matching thread.

On the Beach Crib Coverlet

Every baby needs his own special blanket, and this crib coverlet is the perfect accessory for a coastal room. This throw is a simple block design embroidered with the nautical designs. You can find pre-quilted fabric from a sewing store and embroider the designs inside the blocks for an easy, polished look. It washes easily and is a nice weight for a little child. Choose a contrasting fabric for the trim, and you will have a simple, practical throw to keep baby warm.

Products Needed:

1½ yd. navy blue quilted fabric (measures 40" x 50")
½ yd. light blue binding fabric
½ yd. yellow/blue dot fabric
Target Stickers
Lightweight tear-away stabilizer
Embroidery thread
1 yd. fusible interfacing

On the CD:

Boat #1, Anchor and Lifesaver embroidery designs
Boat #1, Anchor and Lifesaver design templates

On the Beach Crib Coverlet Instructions

1 | Cut the yellow/blue dot fabric into four strips. Two will measure 6" wide x 40" long, and two will measure 6" wide x 50" long. Iron fusible interfacing to all four strips. Place the strips in a block pattern with the top and bottom strips 7" from the edge of the navy blue fabric. Topstitch the two strips in place with matching thread. Lay the remaining two strips perpendicular, 12" from each long side of the navy blue fabric, and topstitch in place. Press.

2 | To make the embroidery process a bit easier, work from the bottom of the coverlet up to the top. You will be rolling the fabric, so the Target Stickers can come off. Place the Anchor and Lifesaver templates in the center of the bottom three blocks. Mark with a target sticker. Embroider the three designs.

3 | Place the Boat #1 template in the large center square. Mark with a Target Sticker in the center. Embroider Boat #1. Use the yellow/blue dot fabric with interfacing on the wrong side.

4 | Repeat Step 3 for the bottom part of the coverlet. Remove all stabilizer from the back of the fabric.

5 | Cut the light blue binding fabric for the binding into 4"-wide strips. The perimeter of the quilt measures 180". You will need to piece together the light-blue fabric to make the binding; add 4" to this measurement. You can trim the excess later. (This is a very easy way to finish a quilt or wall hanging.) Fold the entire length of light-blue fabric in half horizontally. Press with an iron. Stitch the raw edges of the navy-blue fabric with the raw edges of the binding together, right sides together. The fold of the light blue fabric

will be facing toward the inside of the coverlet. Stitch all around the coverlet. Sew the ends of the binding together. Turn the binding over to the back, and stitch in the ditch of the seam. You must "catch" the fold of the binding on the coverlet back.

beautiful butterflies

Beautiful, sheer fabrics are perfect for a whimsical butterfly room. Your little girl's will be fresh and feminine with plenty of color. These particular designs are very versatile. The designs can be embroidered as an appliqué or simple outline stitch on sheer fabric. No resizing or digitizing required! Have fun with the butterfly designs and use your imagination. There's nothing sweeter than a gossamer butterfly room.

Chapter 5

Ribbon-embellished Basket

Here is another way to use embroidered ribbon: place it on a basket liner as an embellishment! These woven baskets and liners are readily available at stores, and you can decorate the liner with a sheer embroidered ribbon. Decide which direction the designs will be, and then embroider butterflies horizontally along the wired ribbon. Lay the ribbon on your basket, and mark where the embroidery will stop. It's pretty and practical!

Products Needed:

2"-wide wired ribbon (length to be determined by basket width)
Lighweight wash-away stabilizer
Masking tape

On the CD:

Butterfly #1 embroidery design

Ribbon-embellished Basket Instructions

1 | Lay the ribbon on your basket, and mark where the embroidery will stop with masking tape. Hoop the wired ribbon in the largest hoop available with the wash-away stabilizer. Repeat design Butterfly #1 as many times as needed to fill the width of the ribbon. If the basket will be viewed from all sides, embroider both sides of the basket. If the basket will be placed in a corner or against the wall, embroider only one side.

2 | 10 repeats were necessary to fill one side of this large basket. Use the tracing feature on your embroidery machine to test the placement of the design. Keep the ribbon as straight as possible in the center of the hoop. Remove the stabilizer, and re-hoop to embroider the entire length of the ribbon.

3 | Remove the hoop from the embroidery machine. Gently tear away the stabilizer from the back of the ribbon. It is not necessary to wash the stabilizer, it will pull away easily.

4 | Stitch the ribbon on the liner in sections. The ribbon was sewn at the top only and folded outward to give it a dimensional look.

Design Tip:

You can remove the wire in the ribbon easily, but the wire adds body and dimension to your basket.

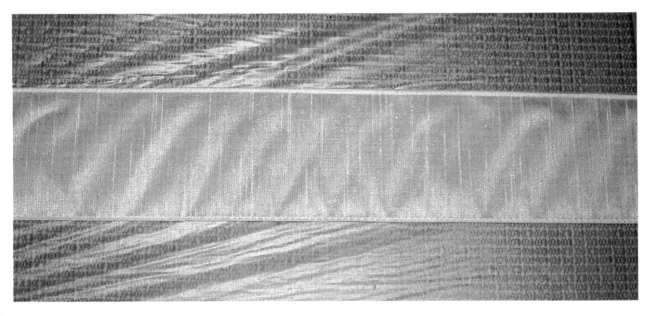

Gossamer Sheer Crib Skirt

I enjoy embroidering on sheer fabrics, but it is a challenge. You will need to properly hoop the wash-away stabilizer and rinse it completely. The sheer fabric dries quickly and looks so elegant. Finish the hem with a "puddle" effect, which will allow it to spill onto the floor. It's perfectly pretty!

Products Needed:

Crib skirt pattern*
Recommended fabric requirements of sheer fabric
Fusible wash-away stabilizer*
Target Stickers

On the CD:

Butterfly #4 embroidery design
Butterfly #4 design template on tracing paper

* Used in this project: Simplicity pattern #4627 (with 3" added to the length), Floriani Fusible stabilizer

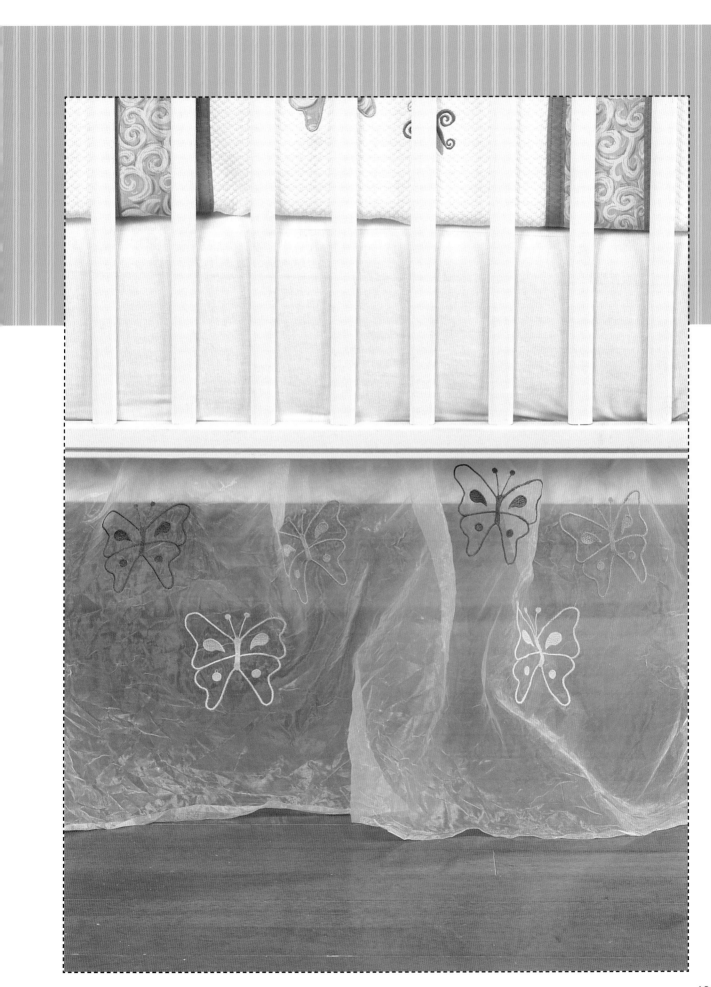

Gossamer Sheer Crib Skirt Instructions

1 | Follow pattern directions for cutting and sewing the crib skirt. All embroidery can be done after construction is complete.

2 | Print four Butterfly #4 design templates.

3 | Butterfly #4 is embroidered as a simple outline stitch, and it is specifically designed for appliqué. You can open the design in editing software and delete the tack-down stitch, or you can manually do that at the machine. Then, move forward to the next color. If you prefer, use the same color in the entire design so no thread color changes are necessary.

4 | Lay the templates on the finished crib skirt at one end. Mark the desired location for each with a target sticker. Hoop as many butterflies as possible at one time. Move along the crib skirt as you complete one area at a time.

5 | After an area is marked with Target Stickers, iron on the stabilizer. Be sure to cut a large enough piece to fit the entire hoop. Start at one end, and move toward the opposite end. Place the designs randomly, and mix up the colors.

6 | After all embroidery is complete, simply rinse the whole crib skirt under cool water. You can lay it in a clean bathtub or sink. I use my hands and gently wash the stabilizer away, then place in the dryer on a low temperature to speed the process. Double-check to see if all the stabilizer has been washed away. Re-wash if necessary.

Design Tip:

Use fusible wash-away stabilizer. A tear-away stabilizer would distort the outline stitches.

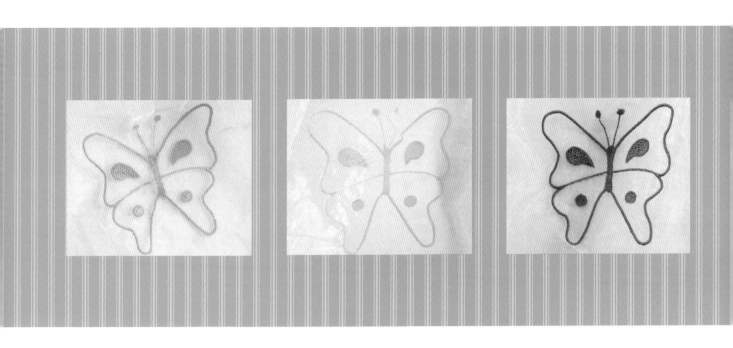

Butterfly Wings Crib Bumpers

These lovely crib bumpers are fresh and bright in white quilted fabric. If you can't find quilted fabric, consider purchasing a queen-size coverlet from a retail store. There was plenty of fabric to make the crib quilt, valance and bumper set. Visit large discount stores and browse through the shower curtains and bedding products. Many ready-made items are the perfect size for a valance and other home decorating accessories.

Products Needed:

1 queen-size coverlet, or approximately 3 yd. home
    decorating fabric
Crib bumper pattern*
2 yd. grosgrain ribbon
Ready-made foam crib bumper pads
½ yd. coordinating fabric
Target Stickers
Fusible interfacing
Medium tear-away stabilizer
Embroidery thread

On the CD:

Butterfly #1 and Butterfly #4 embroidery designs
Butterfly #1 and Butterfly #4 design templates

*Used in this project: Simplicity pattern #4627

Butterfly Wings Crib Bumpers Instructions

1 | Follow pattern directions for crib bumpers, and cut fabric accordingly. Fuse the interfacing to the wrong side of contrasting fabric that will be used for the appliqué butterflies and strips of fabric. The strips of fabric will be used to separate the design groups into sections. Cut six strips of fabric 4" wide x 11½" tall. Place three fabric strips on each long section of bumper pad. Fold one white section of bumper fabric in half vertically, pin one fabric strip in the middle. Topstitch directly on the white fabric (raw edges will be covered with ribbon trim). Measure 12" from the center fabric strip and sew the remaining fabric strips at either end. Follow same directions for opposite long side of bumper pads. There are no fabric strips sewn on the two short ends of the bumper pads.

Cut the grosgrain ribbon into ten 18" lengths. These will be used to fasten the crib bumpers to the crib. Fold the ribbon in half and sew the fold in to the top seam when constructing the bumper pads.

2 | Open the Butterfly #1 and Butterfly #4 designs in editing software. There will be two of Butterfly #1 and one of Butterfly #4. Arrange the designs as shown in the picture. Save this new design as Butterfly 6. Butterfly 6 will be embroidered in four separate locations: two on each long side of the crib bumper, between the fabric sections that were sewn in Step 1.

3 | On one short side, the head of crib bumper, embroider two designs of Butterfly #4. Use the interfaced coordinating fabric, and highlight the elements with matching thread colors. Construct the bumpers and sew four ribbon ties (two on each end) inside the seams to attach to the crib.

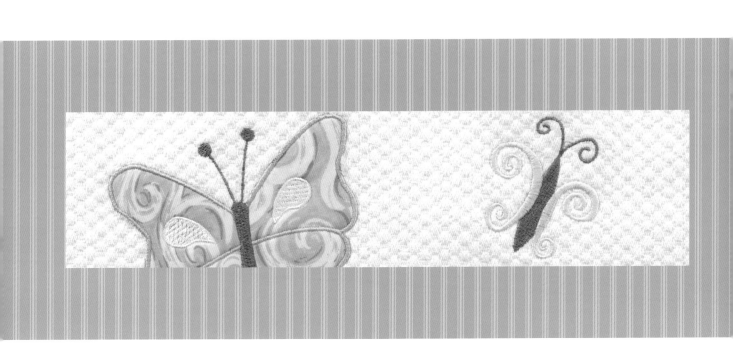

Butterfly Dreams Crib Coverlet

Your baby will dream of floating on the wind under this breezy white coverlet decorated with butterflies. The difference between a coverlet and a quilt is the actual construction. A quilt has three layers sewn together and a binding to finish all raw edges. A coverlet has one layer, and the embroidery can be seen from the back of the coverlet. Use white quilted fabric for this project, or use a purchased queen-size coverlet as I mentioned before.

Products Needed:

40" x 50" piece of white quilted fabric
(2) 35" x 8" strips of coordinating fabric (lime/aqua)
4 yd. large rick-rack trim
½ yd. teal fabric
Medium-weight tear-away stabilizer
Embroidery thread
Fusible interfacing
Target Stickers

On the CD:

Butterfly #4 embroidery design
3 Butterfly #4 design templates

Butterfly Dreams Crib Coverlet Instructions

1 | Iron the fusible interfacing on the contrasting teal and lime/aqua fabric. Take the two long lime/aqua fabric strips and position them 10" from the long edges of white fabric. Keep strips equal in length, they should be 8" from top and bottom edges of white fabric. Topstitch the lime/aqua fabric in place. Raw edges will be covered with rick-rack trim.

2 | Topstitch rick-rack trim on top of the raw edges of lime/aqua fabric. Cut two 20" x 6" pieces of teal fabric for top and bottom sections.

3 | Fold raw edges under ¼", and topstitch in place over the bottom of lime/aqua fabric strips. Press all fabric strips.

4 | All embroidery designs will be stitched as an outline design. The colors have changed for each butterfly. Match your thread color to the coordinating fabric. Fold the quilt in half vertically, and mark the center with a target sticker. Lay the three Butterfly #4 templates on the center of the white fabric. Move the first target sticker and place it with two more for each butterfly. Hoop the white fabric with tear-away stabilizer, and embroider the three butterflies as an outline.

5 | Continue embroidering the remaining six butterflies. Measure 8" from the bottom edge of the teal fabric on the top and bottom sections. Lay the templates on the white fabric, and mark with Target Stickers for the three butterflies. Embroider this group, and follow same directions for bottom group of designs.

6 | Turn coverlet raw edges under ½", and topstitch to finish. Remove all stabilizer from the back.

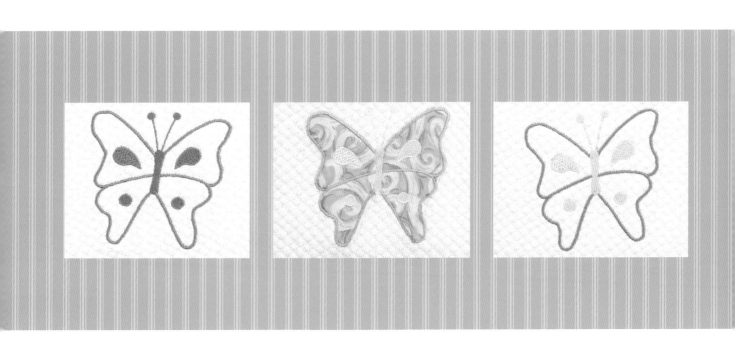

White, Fringed, Butterfly Valance

Let your creativity run wild with this fun project! Measure the window, frame to frame. Decide on the type of rod you will use, the width of the rod and the return (the measurement from the front of the rod to the wall, usually about two or three inches). Add all the measurements together , and add 6" for seams. This valance has a relaxed look — if you prefer ruffles, add more fabric to the width measurement.

To complete the valance, add dimensional butterflies. Embroider appliqué butterflies in the lime/aqua fabric on tulle (bridal netting), and tack them down randomly on the valance.

This valance is 22" long from the top of the rod pocket to the bottom edge. The rod pocket measures 3".

Products Needed:

1½ yd. white quilted fabric
1 yd. lime/aqua coordinating fabric
1½ yd. lime/aqua fringe trim
Target Stickers
¼ yd. white bridal tulle
Water-soluble stabilizer
Medium-weight tear-away stabilizer
Fusible interfacing

On the CD:

Butterfly #4, Butterfly #5 and Butterfly #2 embroidery designs
3 Butterfly #4 design templates
2 Butterfly #5 design templates
1 Butterfly #2 design template

White, Fringed, Butterfly Valance Instructions

1 | Open the Butterfly #5 and Butterfly #2 designs in editing software. Place a Butterfly #2 design on both sides of Butterfly #4, the appliqué butterfly. Save this new design as Butterfly 6. Print a template of new design Butterfly 6.

2 | Iron the fusible interfacing to wrong side of the lime/aqua fabric; this is the appliqué butterfly fabric.

3 | Cut a strip of the lime/aqua fabric about 4" long by width of white fabric needed. Press top and bottom raw edges under and topstitch 2" from top of valance. This segment is the rod pocket.

4 | Fold the white valance fabric in half vertically; mark the center with a target sticker, then fold the fabric in half horizontally. Mark that center spot with a target sticker. The butterfly embroidery designs are in a random and flowing pattern. I started the layout by scattering all the templates on one end of the valance. Move them around as you like — there is no wrong answer! These directions are meant to guide you, but feel free to branch out and be creative. The only location you may want to plan is the center, because it is nice to work outward from a center point.

5 | Embroider the new design, Butterfly 7, in the center spot marked with a Target Sticker. Mark the other locations with Target Stickers. Embroider the Butterfly #5 design left of center, placing two side by side. Change the thread colors to match the aqua/lime fabric.

6 | Lay the templates on the opposite side of the valance, and mark the locations with Target Stickers. Try to embroider the same amount of designs on each side of the valance fabric. The order does not have to be the same — mix up the designs so they look scattered and natural.

7 | Leave room on the white fabric for the dimensional appliqué butterflies. You can easily mark their location with a template and a Target Sticker. Embroider a total of four dimensional appliqué butterfly designs on the valance.

8 | Hoop the white tulle sandwiched between two layers of water-soluble stabilizer in your largest hoop. Use a "repeat" or merging option to embroider three at a time. Rearrange them as needed to fit closely together. Have the interfaced lime/aqua fabric ready for the butterfly appliqué steps.

9 | After all embroidery is complete, remove the tulle from the hoop. Carefully cut the tulle away in large pieces to separate. Trim closely to the stitching line with small, sharp scissors. The tulle and fabric combination will help the design keep its shape. Spray water to remove any water-soluble stabilizer. You do not have to soak or hold underwater.

10 | Tack the 3-D butterflies where the Target Stickers are placed. Topstitch in the butterfly's body with matching thread, and squeeze the wings together to show the 3-D effect.

11 | Add the matching fringe trim to bottom edge of valance. Use matching thread and white thread in the bobbin. Turn the side edges of the white fabric under ½", and sew to finish.

Shimmering Butterfly Sheer

Add beautiful embroidery to a dull window sheer with embroidered butterflies. The method is identical to the sheer embroidered crib skirt. The base of the curtain was sewn with the coordinating lime/aqua fabric. Stitch some of the butterfly embroidery designs as an appliqué, and use others as an outline design. Alternate the colors for a fun, fresh look.

Products Needed:

1 sheer window panel
¾ yd. lime/aqua fabric
Fusible water-soluble stabilizer
Target Stickers
Fusible interfacing

On the CD:

4 Butterfly #4 embroidery designs

Shimmering Butterfly Sheer Instructions

1 | Determine where the embroidery will start on the sheer panel. If using a valance, how far down will it overlap with the sheer panel? Mark the location with a line of chalk or masking tape. You do not want to embroider more than needed if it will not be seen. Place the templates on the sheer fabric under the marked line. Make sure that the layout is random and free. When you are pleased with the position of the butterflies, place a Target Sticker on each spot. Work on one section at a time, top to bottom or side to side. Stagger the appliqué designs with the outline designs.

2 | Iron fusible interfacing to the wrong side of the lime/aqua fabric (enough for four butterflies); set aside for appliqués. Cut the base fabric strip to width of panel and 10" long.

3 | Iron the fusible stabilizer in the desired locations for embroidery. You may have to re-hoop many times because of the distance between the designs. Use a small or medium hoop so you will use less stabilizer. Rinse the embroidered sheer after all designs are complete, and place in dryer on low heat or let air-dry on a hanger.

4 | After the sheer is dry, fold under raw edges of lime/aqua fabric ½" on top and bottom. Topstitch in place; press.

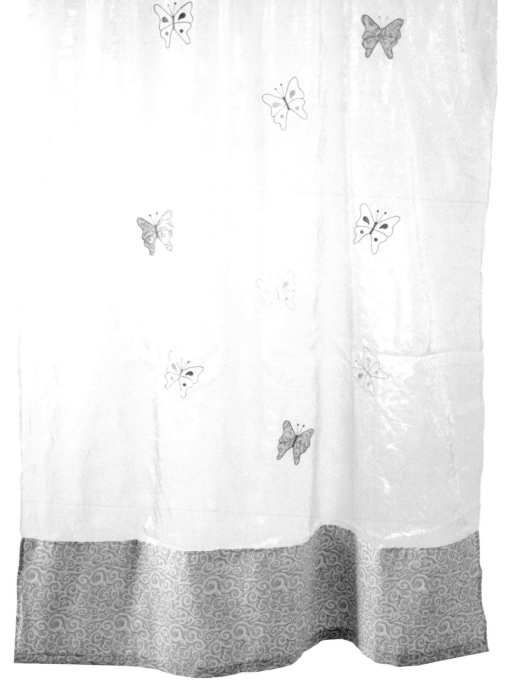

Swirled Diaper Stacker

A ribbon-embellished diaper stacker is another quick and useful project; this stacker was also made from the queen-size coverlet (you can really get your money's worth out of that item!). The stacker fastens to the side of a crib or changing table with a fabric-covered hanger. Instead of embroidering the white fabric directly, you can embroider on two lengths of wired ribbon, and then sew them on the outside front of the stacker. The placement for the embroidery is vertical, as opposed to horizontal for the basket liner.

Products Needed:

Diaper stacker pattern*
1 yd. white fabric
⅜ yd. lime/aqua fabric
⅝ yd. batting or fleece
1 yd. 2"-wide white wired organza ribbon
Water-soluble stabilizer

On the CD:

Butterfly #1 and Butterfly #2 embroidery designs
Butterfly #1 and Butterfly #2 design templates

* Used in this project: Simplicity pattern #4627

Swirled Diaper Stacker Instructions

1 | Open the Butterfly #1 and Butterfly #2 embroidery designs at your machine or software, and position them vertically in the hoop; alternate the designs, and add as many as possible. The designs will be embroidered sideways on the ribbon.

2 | Cut the wired ribbon in half. You will use two pieces of ribbon for the trim. Hoop your largest hoop with water-soluble stabilizer, and place two rows of the ribbon in the hoop.

3 | Use the tracing function to make sure the needle is clear of the wire in the ribbon. Re-hoop if necessary to complete two full lengths of embroidered ribbon. Remove ribbon from hoop, and gently tear away the stabilizer. Rinse under water if the stabilizer does not remove easily.

4 | Follow pattern directions for diaper stacker assembly. Add the embroidered ribbon to the outside of the stacker before sewing the bottom to the front edges.

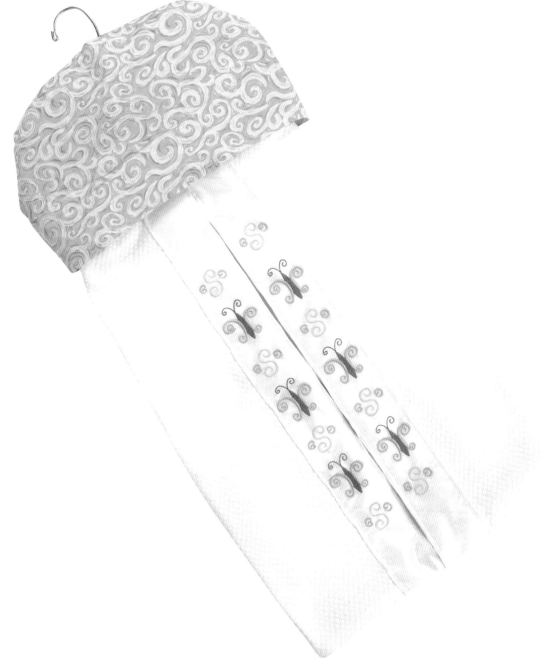

CD Design Index

Airplanes!

Cloud

Plane #1

Plane #3

Plane #4

Plane #5

Flower Garden

Flower #1

Flower #2

Flower #3

Flower #4

Flower #5

Nautical Nursery

Anchor

Boat #1

Lifesaver

Nautical Wheel

Paddle

Beautiful Butterflies

Butterfly #1

Butterfly #2

Butterfly #3

Butterfly #4

Butterfly #5

Resources

All About Blanks, www.allaboutblanks.com

Amazing Designs Smart Sizer Platinum Software, www.amazingdesigns.com

Ann the Gran, www.annthegran.com

Baby Lock Sewing Machines, Designer's Gallery Software, www.babylock.com

Designs in Machine Embroidery Magazine, www.dzgns.com

 In the Hoop by Eileen Roche

 Perfect Placement Kit

 Target Stickers

Directors chairs, www.directorschairs.com

Floriani Stabilizers, www.floriani.com

Internet Embroidery, www.netemb.com

Joann's Craft Store, www.joann.com

McCall's Patterns, www.mccall.com

Microsoft Windows, www.microsoft.com

Nancy's Notions, www.nancysnotions.com

Robison-Anton, www.robison-anton.com

Steve Woods Photography, Dallas, TX

About the Author

This is Marie Zinno's first book on embroidery for children's décor and accessories. She has been a contributing editor for Designs in Machine Embroidery Magazine for three years. Although she enjoys embroidering for babies and children, her home-based custom embroidery business is very diverse. Her specialty is sewing custom purses and tote bags. She has brought her passion to the homes of many Canton, Ohio, women and shares her love of original purses. Her company, Sew Creative Embroidery, is growing quickly.

Make it All About ME

Embroidery Machine Essentials
Appliqué Techniques
by Mary Mulari

This exciting new book gives you more embroidery opportunities and techniques to make the most of your machine. Learn to make beautiful appliqué designs for quilts, garments and gifts.

Softcover • 8¼ x 10⅞ • 48 page 100 color photos and illus.

Item# EMA
$19.99

Fill in the Blanks with Machine Embroidery
by Rebecca Kemp Brent

This innovative guide walks you through basic and essential details about dealing with blanks. With tips and advice about choosing threads and stabilizers, how to locate blanks and techniques to use with specific projects, you'll quickly grow your machine embroidery advantages.

Softcover • 8¼ x 10⅞ • 48 pages 125 color photos

Item# Z0747
$24.99

Machine Embroidery for Special Occasions
by Joan Hinds

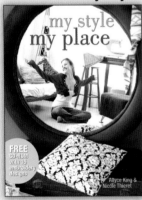

Identify fresh ideas for decorating your world from the 40+ projects based on themes including a birthday party, a day at the beach and a New Year's celebration, featured in this book. Plus, you receive a bonus CD-ROM with 40 embroidery designs.

Softcover • 8¼ x 10⅞ • 128 pages 200+ color photos

Item# Z0748
$29.99

Embroidery Machine Essentials
Fleece Techniques
by Nancy Cornwell

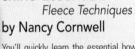

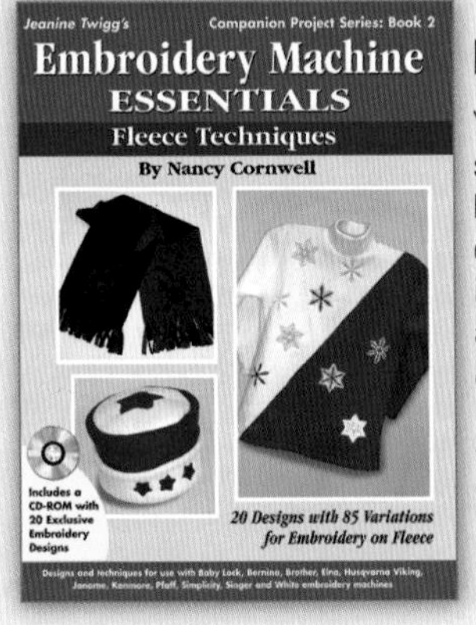

You'll quickly learn the essential how to skills of machine embroidery success, before expanding into new territories with embroidery designs that call on techniques including trapunto effects, "embossing," appliqué, and other means to use embroidery and fleece to create surface texture.

Softcover • 8¼ x 10⅞ • 48 pages Color throughout

Item# EMSF
$19.95

My Style My Place
by Allyce King and Nicole Thieret

With humorous stories, easy-to-follow instructions for 30 quick do-it-yourself projects, and serious support for creativity and individuality, this book appeals to your youthful attitude and desire to express your own spirit in your sewing. Bonus CD-ROM with 20 designs included.

Softcover • 8¼ x 10⅞ • 128 pages 125 color photos

Item# Z0935
$24.99